T0331978

International Equilibrium
and Bretton Woods

International Equilibrium and Bretton Woods

Kalecki's Alternative to Keynes and White and its Consequences

Edited by

JERZY OSIATYŃSKI
JAN TOPOROWSKI

OXFORD
UNIVERSITY PRESS

OXFORD
UNIVERSITY PRESS

Great Clarendon Street, Oxford, OX2 6DP,
United Kingdom

Oxford University Press is a department of the University of Oxford.
It furthers the University's objective of excellence in research, scholarship,
and education by publishing worldwide. Oxford is a registered trade mark of
Oxford University Press in the UK and in certain other countries

Published in the United States of America by Oxford University Press
198 Madison Avenue, New York, NY 10016, United States of America

British Library Cataloguing in Publication Data
Data available

Library of Congress Control Number: 2021951972

ISBN 978–0–19–285640–1
DOI: 10.1093/oso/9780192856401.001.0001

Printed and bound by
CPI Group (UK) Ltd, Croydon, CR0 4YY

Cover image: tony4urban/Shutterstock.com

Acknowledgements

The authors wish to express their deep gratitude to His Excellency Aleksander Surdej, the Permanent Representative of the Republic of Poland at the Organisation for Economic Co-operation and Development for his initiative in organizing the conference on which this volume is based; Professor Elżbieta Mączyńska, Chair of the Polish Economic Society, for her support of the conference, to participants in this conference, Peter Clarke, Stephany Griffith-Jones, Esteban Pérez Caldentey, His Excellency Erdem Başçi, the Permanent Representative of the Republic of Turkey at the OECD, Luiz de Mello, Cyrille Schwellnus, Konrad Sobański and Aleksander Sulejewicz, Patrycja Guzikowska, Mateusz Guzikowski, Robert Matusiak, Marta Postuła, Jarosław Klepacki, Marta Wajda-Lichy and Paweł Kawa, and to Noemi Levy-Orlik, and Matias Vernengo for their contributions to this volume.

A notable absentee from the conference was the distinguished economist Julio López Gallardo, who was known to many of the participants in the conference as a well-known exponent of Kalecki's international and development economics. Participants in the conference received with great sorrow, a few months later, news of his death. Julio López had studied with Kalecki in the 1960s and had in López's work sustained discussion around the Polish economist's work on international economics, most recently in his book with Michaël Assous on Kalecki. Julio López generously agreed to co-author with Hanna Szymborska a chapter that we are now able to include in this volume. The editors wish to acknowledge the kindness of Julio López and his family, as well as the assistance of Hanna Szymborska in realizing his contribution to this volume.

Additional thanks go to Adam Swallow and editors at Oxford University Press.

Finally, our most heartfelt thanks go to Elżbieta Osiatyńska and Anita Prażmowska.

At the proofs stage of this book, Jerzy Osiatyński passed away. The surviving editor and authors of this volume acknowledge his generous contribution and inspiration.

Contents

List of Figures and Tables

Figures

Tables

List of Contributors

Peter Clarke is Emeritus Professor of Modern British History at Cambridge University and a Fellow of the British Academy. His book, *The Keynesian Revolution in the Making, 1924–1936*, was published by Oxford University Press in 1988 and is still in print. His short book, *Keynes: The Twentieth Century's Most Influential Economist*, was published by Bloomsbury in London and New York in 2009.

Stephany Griffith-Jones is Emeritus Professorial Fellow at the Institute for Development Studies, Sussex University, Financial Markets Director, IPD, Columbia University, Non-Resident Fellow at the Center for Global Development and Distinguished Fellow at the ClimateWorks Foundation; she has also worked for many international organizations, as well as national governments. Stephany Griffith-Jones has published over 25 books and numerous articles on international and development finance, as well as macroeconomic and domestic financial issues. She co-directs a research network on development banks, which led to a major conference in 2020 linked to the first summit on development banks.

Noemi Levy-Orlik is a Senior Professor, Economic Faculty, Universidad Nacional Autónoma de México, Mexico City, Mexico. She specializes in money, finance, macroeconomics, and economic development.

Julio López Gallardo died in July 2020. He had retired as Professor of Economics at the Universidad Nacional Autónoma de México and was a member of the Sistema Nacional de Investigadores of Mexico. He was the author, with Michaël Assous, of *Michal Kalecki* (Basingstoke: Palgrave, 2010).

Jerzy Osiatyński is Professor of Economics at the Institute of Economics of the Polish Academy of Sciences and the editor of Collected Works of Michał Kalecki, vols I–VII, (Oxford: Clarendon Press, 1990–97).

Esteban Pérez Caldentey is Chief of the Development Financing Unit (Economic Development Division), Economic Commission for Latin America and the Caribbean (Santiago, Chile); co-editor of the Review of Keynesian Economics and the New Palgrave Dictionary of Economics. Co-author of several publications on Raúl Prebisch.

Hanna Szymborska is a Senior Lecturer in Economics at Birmingham City University, UK. She has previously worked at the Open University and the UK Civil Service, and completed her PhD at the University of Leeds. Her research focuses on wealth, inequality, macroeconomic policy, and financialization. She has published in peer reviewed journals, blogs, and magazines, and has also contributed to edited volumes.

Jan Toporowski is Professor of Economics and Finance at SOAS University of London and Visiting Professor of Economics at Meiji University, Tokyo. He is the author of two volumes of biography of Michał Kalecki.

Matias Vernengo is Professor of Economics at Bucknell University, co-editor of the Review of Keynesian Economics and the New Palgrave Dictionary of Economics. Research interests are in development macroeconomics, international political economy, and history of economic thought.

Introduction

Kalecki's Alternative to Keynes and White and its Consequences

Jerzy Osiatyński and Jan Toporowski

The date of 18 April 2020 marked 50 years from the death of Michał Kalecki. This anniversary was remembered with conferences discussing Kalecki's economics and its present day relevance. The Permanent Representation of the Republic of Poland to the Organisation for Economic Co-operation and Development (OECD) together with the Polish Economic Society organized a conference in Paris to commemorate this anniversary as well as the previous year's seventy-fifth anniversary of the Bretton Woods conference. The subject of the conference was 'Michał Kalecki and the Problem of International Equilibrium' and was held on 26 September 2019. This book brings together some of the papers presented at the OECD conference. The papers, from a number of distinguished speakers, assess the background and the results of the Bretton Woods agreements. The discussion is focused around the critical assessment of the Keynes and White plans by Michał Kalecki, and the consequences of this for present-day international economics and international monetary and financial policy.

There is a huge literature on the Bretton Woods conference. In general this can be grouped into official and unofficial histories of the Bretton Woods institutions; and assessments of the Keynes and White plans that preceded the conference. None of these considers the criticisms that were made of the Keynes and White plans from outside the circle of Keynes and White. Both the International Monetary Fund (IMF) and the World Bank have published much historical material about Bretton Woods and the evolution of policies and procedures since then, and critical evaluations of the operations of the IMF and the World Bank by authors like Richard Peet (2009) are valuable

Jerzy Osiatyński and Jan Toporowski, *Introduction: Kalecki's Alternative to Keynes and White and its Consequences*. In: *International Equilibrium and Bretton Woods*. Edited by Jerzy Osiatyński and Jan Toporowski, Oxford University Press. © Oxford University Press (2022). DOI: 10.1093/oso/9780192856401.003.0001 reflections on the outcome of Bretton Woods. However, these authors have not joined this up to the critical evaluations of the Keynes and White plans at that time: The Bretton Woods arrangements are deemed to have emerged from the two plans. By implication, therefore, critical assessments made of those plans at the time are reckoned to have classed them as irrelevant failures. Among the more recent critical literature, post-Keynesian authors such as Paul Davidson and Robert Skidelsky have assessed Bretton Woods as a gladiatorial contest between Keynes and White, to the neglect of the criticisms of both plans that highlighted the actual principles behind them. This volume brings together the critical assessments that were made at the time—by Kalecki, Ernst Schumacher, Thomas Balogh, and Raúl Prebisch—and virtually unknown today, together with critical examination of the work of the Bretton institutions since that time.

Michał Kalecki[1] was born in Łódź on 22 June 1899, a single child in a middle class Jewish family. In 1913 he witnessed the bankruptcy of his father's spinning mill and, in 1925, of his uncle's large shipping company where his father worked after having lost his own business. The young Kalecki studied engineering at Gdańsk Technical University (he had started studying engineering in 1917 in Warsaw), but he was forced to leave Gdańsk and return to Łódź to support his father financially. Self-taught in economics, in 1927 he moved to Warsaw where he earned his living partly by publishing business reviews in Polish economic periodicals. In 1929, he started a permanent job at the Institute for the Study of Business Cycles and Prices, a government think-tank in Warsaw. In 1933, the institute published his *Essay on the Business Cycle Theory* (1933 [1990]), in which he not only laid out the theoretical foundations for the cyclical nature of capital accumulation, but also—together with his other papers—set out the core of what was later recognized as his original version of the theory of effective demand. In 1934 and 1935, together with Ludwik Landau, Kalecki published the first estimates of the national income of Poland in 1929 and in 1933, i.e. at the beginning and the end of the world 1929–33 economic crisis.[2] The unique feature of those estimates was that they revealed the functional distribution of Poland's aggregate national income between profits and wages in those years (and

---

[1] This section borrows from Osiatyński 2017. Next to his biographical Introduction to Vol. 1 of Kalecki's *Collected Works* (Kalecki 1990) and 'The Dates and Facts in Kalecki's Life' (in Kalecki 1997), there are many intellectual biographies of Kalecki, chronologically starting with Feiwel 1975, to Łaski 1987, Lopez and Assous 2010, Toporowski 2013 and 2018, and Osiatyński 2017, among others.

[2] Published in 1934 and 1935 respectively, see Kalecki 1996; see also Osiatyński's editorial notes therein, pp. 554–5.

that they also spelled out some methodological guidelines for making national income estimates). The macroeconomic essence of those estimates, which were among the first calculations of the volume of national income ever made in the world, is that the distribution of gross national income between profits and wages was implicitly linked to Kalecki's macroeconomic business cycle theory which had gross aggregate investments determining gross profits which in turn determine cyclical fluctuations of gross national income and employment.

Following the French and English publications of summaries of his 1933 *Essay* (Kalecki 1933 [1990]), and its presentation at the Econometric Society conference in Leyden, in late 1935, Kalecki was granted a Rockefeller Foundation fellowship. In February 1936 he went to Sweden and shortly after Keynes's *General Theory of Employment, Interest and Money* was published he moved to London. The end of that year marks the first of his protest-resignations—against the disciplinary firing from the Warsaw Institute of his two close friends who had written a critical commentary on government policy. In England he met Keynes, Joan Robinson, and other members of the Keynes's inner circle. Although the relationship between Kalecki and Keynes evoked mixed feelings on both sides, when, in 1938, Kalecki's Rockefeller fellowship ended Keynes arranged a research job for him in the Department of Economics in Cambridge thus allowing the Kaleckis to postpone their return to Poland shortly before the outbreak of World War Two (WWII), which they would not have survived.

In 1939 Kalecki published *Essays in the Theory of Economic Fluctuations* which focused on filling gaps in Keynes's short-term theory, on its refinement and statistical corroboration, and on integrating it with his own theory of business cycles. The book earned Kalecki the status of Keynes's student and follower, although in fact he independently formulated the theory of effective demand and maintained his own version of it.

During the war Kalecki worked at the Oxford University Institute of Economics and Statistics which gave shelter to many economists who had escaped fascism in their native European countries. He soon became the institute's guru in its research and publications on the British war economy and on ways to secure full employment in the course of post-war reconstruction. This work gave rise among others to his involvement in the debate on post-war arrangements that would assist maintaining full employment together with equilibrium in multilateral trade and capital movements. In 1943 he published his *Studies in Economic Dynamics* in which he combined his business cycle theory with long-run growth.

After the war Kalecki worked for a year in the International Labour Office, and spent a few months in Warsaw advising the Polish Government. From the end of 1946 he worked at the Economic Department of the UN Secretariat. In the UN, he supervised annual reports on inflationary and deflationary tendencies, reports on full employment policies, but first and foremost the annual *World Economic Report* series. In 1954 his *Theory of Economic Dynamics* was published. In the atmosphere of McCarthyism and with his responsibilities at the UN Secretariat being increasingly constrained, he resigned in protest from his job in the UN at the end of 1954. In early 1955 he returned to Poland to assume a high-ranking advisory position to the government, in the Planning Commission.

In his work on centrally planned economies, Kalecki concentrated on problems of annual and long-run plans of Poland's development, on proportions of growth of investment and consumption, and on a system of economic management that would harmonize central planning with market mechanism measures. This work gave rise to his 1963 *Introduction to the Theory of Growth in a Socialist Economy*. Critical of setting overambitious economic growth rate targets, Kalecki's advice was increasingly ignored by the political authorities, eventually again leading to his resignation from his responsibility for long-term planning.

Kalecki's academic and policy influence in Poland did not last long. Political infighting in the leadership of the Polish Communist Party in 1967–68 was intertwined with anti-Semitic motives. Many of Kalecki's friends and collaborators were dismissed from their jobs and forced to emigrate. Kalecki's economic theory was heavily criticized in a series of politically orchestrated conferences. Kalecki considered the argument presented in the conference papers of his critics: 'verbose, vague, and their economic reasoning [of] low standard'. Following these developments, Kalecki once again submitted his resignation and took early retirement. On 18 April 1970 he passed away. A couple of months after the March 1968 purges, his Warsaw circle ceased to exist, although his ideas continued to develop in the work of his former students and collaborators who emigrated from Poland (Kazimierz Łaski and Ignacy Sachs among them). Together with western heterodox economists they continued to develop the theories of Kalecki and Keynes thus contributing to the post-Kaleckian and post-Keynesian schools of economics.

Part I of this volume examines theoretical and practical foundations of White's and Keynes's respective plans for establishing the post-WWII international monetary system at Bretton Woods in the context of a political pledge of securing and maintaining full employment. This provides the context for Kalecki's criticisms of those plans and suggestions for reinforcing full employment policies. This, it will be argued, was a critical difference between the positions of Keynes and White, and the suggestions of their Oxford critics. Keynes and White took the view that full employment policies could be fitted into a functioning international payments system, once arrangements had been made for resolving 'temporary' balance of payments of disequilibria. By contrast Kalecki and his colleagues recognized that the very compulsion to restore external equilibrium was a way of forcing disequilibrium onto the domestic economy in the form of unemployment and below-capacity production. Once economies are obliged to maintain external balance, for a given propensity to import employment comes to be determined by exports, in the standard relationship that is now familiar from the work of Anthony Thirlwall (Thirlwall 1979).

Chapter 1 by Jerzy Osiatyński reviews Kalecki's ideas on how to handle the problem of balance of payments equilibrium while pursuing the policy of achieving and maintaining full employment. He also examines the essence of Kalecki's proposal to extend the Keynes plan in order to establish a mechanism that would facilitate long-term funding of investment for deficit countries. An account of Kalecki's practical experience, a few years later and largely unknown, in the context of his supervising of the United Nations reports on full employment policies pursued by individual UN member countries is also given here. This experience supports Kalecki's 1943 concerns regarding practical measures available to governments to defend balance of trade positions and confirms his criticism of the Keynes–White plans.

Throughout all his life, the achievement and maintenance of full employment was the key issue which Kalecki addressed whether in the context of a capitalist economy, a strictly centrally-planned one, or a developing economy. Full employment was of critical relevance for economic policymaking in his time, as it is at present. However, it was not the central question addressed by Keynes and White or by others who at the time discussed the foundations of Bretton Woods institutions. Their agenda was broadly set by the free-trade doctrine according to which unrestrained world trade was a powerful growth engine for all trading partners. Their concern was to establish an international payments system to replace gold payments and a mechanism to secure international balance of payment equilibrium without individual countries resorting to export promotion, import substitution, or deflationary economic policy instruments.

In Chapter 2 Peter Clarke explores the background and origins of the Keynes plan, and of the rival White plan, from 1941 onwards, and explains how their two authors reached a compromise on the proposals that became the agenda for the Bretton Woods conference in 1944; if compromise it was. An established critic of the gold standard, John Maynard Keynes was aware that its functioning before World War One (WWI) in clearing international balances had required leading countries to be able to enforce 'the rules of the game' on other trading partners as well as being able to provide credit to countries experiencing deficits in their international balances. Keynes's concept of the International Clearing Union (ICU) was to deliver that, and to avoid the deflationary policies used before WWII to protect individual countries' competitive positions. The ICU was the device to enable smooth settlement of foreign balances for all trading countries in a way that would promote further liberalization of foreign trade. Keynes also knew that foreign borrowing during WWI left Great Britain—notwithstanding its special relations with the British Empire—as a descending hegemon in deciding the terms of clearing international transactions, and that the ascending hegemonic position could be taken at the time only by the net creditor country at the end of WWII, the United States. 'In 1929', Keynes wrote in 1930, 'the net surplus of our foreign balance ... was greater last year than that of any other country, being indeed 50% greater than the corresponding surplus of the United States' (Keynes 1930 [1963]: 359). By 1943 he was only too aware that the respective position of the two countries had completely reversed.

Both, Harry Dexter White and Keynes were heavily committed to free trade and economic liberalism that greatly facilitated compromise. As the price of that compromise the United States conceded the continuation of Britain's special trading arrangements with its empire, which Keynes strongly and successfully defended, although they were an offence to the doctrine of free trade. Clarke's essay provides support to Jan Toporowski's claim (pp. 61–63 in Chapter 3 of this volume) that for the two main actors of the debate and founders of the Bretton Woods institutions, the constraints on poorer countries' economic development posed by its dependence on imports were of minor importance. The attention of Keynes and White was focused on expanding world trade, which they considered the key vehicle to achieving and maintaining full employment. They did not consider criticism from outside the diplomatic circle of the government delegations invited to Bretton Woods, in particular the comments put forward in 1943–44 by Kalecki and the group of Oxford University economists, nor did they appreciate fully the consequences of the Bretton Woods system for developing countries, then still colonies or without voice in the discussions of the war-time allies.

In his chapter, Toporowski shows how the Oxford critique of Kalecki, Thomas Balogh, and Ernst Schumacher rested on a complex understanding of the multilateral payments system that would be required to support any expansion of international trade. This analysis points to the problems that have plagued the international monetary system since Bretton Woods: the breakdown of multilateralism in 1948; the continuing debt problems of developing countries; the excessive dependence on the US dollar; and the emergence of regionalism in trade and monetary arrangements. An important corollary that follows from Chapters 1 and 3 from Osiatyński and Toporowski respectively relates to the conceptual difference in the meaning of equilibrium for White and Keynes on the one hand, and for Kalecki, Schumacher, and Balogh on the other hand. For the former, balance of payments equilibrium is available at full employment, at least in the medium and long-run. True, for Keynes, as well as for the ardent New-Dealer— Harry White—that equilibrium could also be at less than full employment, in which case government intervention was necessary.

This is not the theoretical framework of Kalecki, who saw the market economy oscillating along a rising trend line, due to technical progress, but with its dynamics determined by aggregate demand. In the absence of sufficient aggregate private spending to secure lasting full employment, government spending is needed. A fiscal deficit becomes necessary when intended private investment is less than intended private savings, in the absence of net exports. Deficit spending is a policy measure to protect against the cumulative adjustment of private investment and private savings through reduced output, employment, and thereby of profits and household incomes from which savings can be made.

For Kalecki, each country should follow its own effective policy of full employment based predominantly on domestic resources. But this did not mean that foreign trade balances could be obtained at full employment levels of output. What measures could be taken—asked Kalecki and Schumacher in their 1943 paper—should any country face persistent deficit in its balance of payments due to inadequate exports to cover the import requirements at full employment, in order to avoid deflationary adjustment and abandonment of the full employment policy target? Full employment, they thought, could be sustained if Keynes's ICU was supplemented by an affiliated investment bureau whose credit activity would assure availability to deficit countries of the foreign exchange of countries which experience chronic export surpluses. Thus international liquidity would be maintained in the system. There is not much room for an automatic adjustment to equilibrium by means of market mechanism alone, they argued, and full employment policy needs to be supported by government net spending on the one hand and on the other by an international institution that would provide foreign liquidity for countries with chronic net imports. Their scepticism that exchange rate adjustment could provide foreign trade equilibrium was to be borne out in the studies which showed imports and exports to be insufficiently elastic with respect to the exchange rate (the Marshall–Lerner conditions) to secure that equilibrium.

Part I of the volume closes with an account of a related critical response to the Bretton Woods discussions, that of the Argentine economist, Raúl Prebisch. Esteban Pérez Caldentey and Matías Vernengo outline in Chapter 4 Prebisch's three key objections to the Keynes plan, namely that: (i) it could lead to inflationary pressures; (ii) it did not appreciate the differences between the centre and the periphery in terms of international power and economic structure and that achieving full employment in the United States would not ensure international equilibrium but would rather create an external imbalance in the countries of the periphery (p. 82 below); and (iii) under the Keynes and White plans pursuing full employment in the periphery would be difficult; the high import requirements of countries in the periphery would necessarily entail a balance-of-payments disequilibrium which could not be adjusted either by beggar-thy-neighbour policies (exchange rate devaluations), or through the Gold Standard rules of the game (contraction of internal demand), with the only feasible alternative being exchange controls which, however, were not allowed under the Keynes and White plans.

On all those points Prebisch's position was close to that of Kalecki and the Oxford critique of the Keynes–White Bretton Woods compromise. These similarities are well seen when Pérez and Vernengo's account of Prebish's contribution to the first UN Conference on Trade and Development (Geneva 1964) is compared with what Kalecki wrote on the economic development of countries in Africa, Asia and Latin America. Similar concerns to those of Prebisch appear in Kalecki's writings on developing economies (see Kalecki 1963 [1993]). What then were the differences between them? They will be seen in Kalecki's involvement in preparing in 1963 the official Polish position for the UNCTAD conference. It took place when membership of the United Nations rapidly increased:

'as colonies achieved independence in the years after the Second World War, had raised the profile and the influence of developing countries in the UN through representative bodies such as the UN's General Assembly. This was a challenge to the supremacy of the United States outside the Soviet bloc, where the American government was handicapped by its Cold War policies supporting military dictatorships in Latin America and Asia.'

(Toporowski 2018: 230)

Having by then developed his concepts of 'mixed economies' (Kalecki 1963 [1993]) and of 'intermediate regimes' (Kalecki 1964 [1993]) Kalecki put forward his system of perspective planning as a way of mapping out sustainable economic and social development for developing countries, and his proposal largely became the Polish official position. Since 1962 Kalecki had been running a seminar on problems and methods of constructing optimum five-year plans in various model-types of less developed economies. The participants included his teaching assistants and postgraduate students as well as research staff and economic policy practitioners from less developed countries. In preparing those plans Kalecki recommended taking into account the specific natural environment and endowment of each country under examination. In his famous 'planning games' (see Osiatyński 1993: 191–192), he distinguished three types of countries: (i) those that could produce world-traded agricultural products ('cocoaland countries'); (ii) oil-rich countries; and (iii) countries that could base their development on extensive cattle-breeding. In their long-term development plans each country had to rely first of all on its domestic resources, including financial capital, and on satisfying the needs of low-income social classes. The prime engine of development was the perspective plan combined with market mechanisms. Prebisch would not go as far as that.

Part II of this volume takes the discussion from 1944 to the present day, to cover some of the developments in the international monetary system that exposed the limitations of the settlements agreed at Breton Woods, and to examine the relevance of Kalecki's ideas on multilateralism and full employment in the twenty-first century. While the early years of the Bretton Woods system demonstrated the difficulties of maintaining fixed exchange rates, even with the option of adjustment, from the 1980s onwards problems in the system came to be concentrated on the credit and debt relations between the 'periphery' and the core capitalist countries. This part opens with Chapter 5 by Noemi Levy-Orlik, who argues that the post-war financial organization (the Bretton Woods system) could not deliver overall economic stability because international liquidity rested on a national currency (the US dollar) that performed the role of international money, which meant the US economy had to run permanent balance of payments deficits to secure worldwide liquidity. The structure of fixed but adjustable exchange rates failed to guarantee the necessary liquidity for international trade. Moreover, it was not accompanied by financial instruments to guarantee financial stability, and long-term loans were insufficient to finance the development of backward regions. For these reasons the Bretton Woods multilateral system failed, and beggar-thy-neighbour practices reappeared along with unregulated international money markets (e.g. the Eurodollar market), seeding destabilization of the international financial system. These developments set the stage for a new international financial order based on globalized and transnational economic structures of a highly unstable nature. The post-Bretton Woods financial system, she argues, is presently dominated by private debt, unrelated to any commodity, and provides unlimited space for the circulation of capital not related to savings. In this environment, private capital flows and capital markets largely affect exchange rates and the induced financial inflation changes the distribution of profits in favour of large corporations and big capital. The reappearance of private debt at the international level has deepened external trade disequilibria and reactivated capital markets in developed countries, but less so in the developing countries that are supposed to benefit from globalization. Under these settings, Latin American economies generated *sui generis* conditions that combined excess liquidity in international currency with increasing economic dependency, and limited finance for actual economic development.

Levy-Orlik's chapter is followed by Stephany Griffith-Jones's consideration in Chapter 6 of how domestic investment may be effectively financed to support full employment. Investment plays a key role in the respective theoretical frameworks of Keynes and Kalecki as the key determinant of output, productivity, and employment. Because of its significance also for future output and employment, the key problem for economic policymakers in emerging and developing economies is to ensure sufficient volume of investment, and in particular to ensure long-term financing of fixed-capital investment. For the reasons spelled out by Kalecki and the Oxford critics of the Keynes plan, possibilities of supplying such long-term credits for developing economies were severely limited under the arrangements of Bretton Woods institutions. This role, argues Griffith-Jones, was taken over and expanded by national and regional development banks. For instance, under the Juncker Plan, the European Investment Bank (EIB) was to be additionally capitalized between 2015 and 2020 by about €500 billion, which with ten-fold leverage could hugely increase its long-term financing of the private sector as well as public investment without infringing the European Monetary Union's limits on fiscal financing. Providing liquidity to the EIB did not prove a spectacular success in terms of increasing private investment in fixed capital, since private investment depends more on expected profitability and other factors. But as shown in Griffith-Jones's chapter (and in her and José Antonio Ocampo's 2018 book *The Future of National Development Banks*), in the context of emerging and developing countries these banks significantly facilitated financing long-term investment projects.

This is followed in Chapter 7 by Hanna Szymborska with Julio López Gallardo, who ask the question if a new Bretton Woods agreement could be effective in stimulating economic prosperity around the world today and if so, under what conditions could this be accomplished? Szymborska is sceptical about the possibility of such an agreement and she argues that it:

'could not be easily transplanted into the modern context due to several fundamental differences characterizing the state of the global economy today and in the mid-1940s. At present, international economic cooperation faces an overwhelming challenge of radically rethinking the ideological tenets on which the dominant approach to economic policy is based. This would require learning from the insights of Kalecki and Keynes in order to realign policy priorities in the global economy away from the neoclassical emphasis on maintaining price stability and promoting individual profit opportunities towards inclusive stimulation of aggregate demand. Such an approach would create opportunities for nurturing global economic prosperity that is not only more socially just but also environmentally sustainable.'

A key difference is that the 1940s war-time economies had virtually full employment, and social inequalities were repressed by the needs of war finance and the subsequent post-war recovery, and the memory of the Great Depression. The political consensus in favour of high employment and social equality is missing today.

In the final chapter of this volume Jan Toporowski (Chapter 8) argues that in the twenty-first century the dominant force in the international monetary system is no longer trade but international debt, which makes developing countries into the weakest link in the international monetary system. Any possibility of equilibrium is frustrated by capital flows that, for the poorer developing countries, are driven by unstable commodity prices. Capital flows are further destabilized by the international monetary cycles derived from monetary policy in the United States. Many critics have argued that this can be overcome by a return to controls on foreign capital flows. However, Toporowski argues that this is not feasible given the preponderance of private sector cross-border debt. Instead the chapter advocates reduced reliance on foreign borrowing and increasing domestic borrowing, where Kalecki argued that debt management may be more effective. Such long-term borrowing can support more effective use of fiscal policy as well as the institutional mechanisms suggested by Griffith-Jones.

Arguably the most important innovation of the twenty-first century in the international monetary system has been the system of currency swaps by which the Federal Reserve System maintains the international monetary stability of selected central banks (Shirakawa 2021). This prevented an international financial crisis in 2008, and again in 2020 with the Covid pandemic, and has provided the liquidity to allow governments in wealthy countries to absorb the costs of the pandemic. However, developing countries have largely been excluded from this currency safety net. They carry with them the burden not only of the pandemic, but also one of renewed debt.

It was not only the specific needs of developing countries that were neglected, if not actually overlooked, in the White plan and, eventually, in the Bretton Woods agreements, where those countries had little voice. Their position was put by the critics of those agreements in Oxford and elsewhere. Kalecki in particular saw the difficulties of sustaining multilateral Keynesianism not only for countries in need of industrialization, but also for countries whose capital structure did not allow for balanced trade at full employment. A review of the Oxford critique of the Keynes and White plans sheds additional light on the hitherto unknown history of Bretton Woods arrangements, their shortfalls and achievements, and the fundamental principles of international monetary and financial economics.

A reform of the international monetary system today must start from a reconsideration of the fault lines of the present system. Kalecki was remarkably prescient in seeing the fault lines of the system in his time and identifying the elements necessary for an efficient international payments system, to back up free trade and multilateralism, defined as the ability to use a payment from one country to settle obligations in another country. He recognized that full employment carries no guarantee of trade balance, because capital is not distributed among countries in such a way as to support employment, and market forces cannot bring about the necessary redistribution, even if neoclassical economics promises an eventual future of trade balance at full employment: Keynes had rightly criticized this with his early observation that '… this *long run* is a misleading guide to current affairs. *In the long run* we are all dead. Economists set themselves too easy, too useless a task if in tempestuous seasons they tell us that when the storm is long past the ocean is flat again'. (Keynes 1923: 80). Along with Keynes, Kalecki recognized that attempts to obtain trade balance through reductions in real wages could only bring social strife and the revulsion against free trade and multilateralism that runs through populism from the nineteenth century, through the inter-war years in which the views of Keynes and Kalecki were formed, up to the present day. Both had come to the view that an alternative to the Gold Standard was necessary to support free trade and multilateralism but was not sufficient. But Kalecki went further than Keynes in seeing the need for long-term investment planning and, to support that, a system of long-term credit to avoid dependence on the 'tempestuous seasons' of capital markets.

References

Feiwel, George R. 1975 *The Intellectual Capital of Michał Kalecki: A Study in Economic Theory and Policy*. Knoxville: TN: University of Tennessee Press.

Griffith-Jones, Stephany and Juan Antonio Ocampo 2018 (eds.) *The Future of National Development Banks*. Oxford: Oxford University Press.

Kalecki, Michał 1933 [1990] 'Essay on the Business Cycle Theory', in Jerzy Osiatyński (ed.) *Collected Works of Michał Kalecki. Volume I Capitalism: Business Cycles and Full Employment*. Oxford: Clarendon Press. pp. 65–109.

Kalecki, Michał 1939 [1990] 'Essays in the Theory of Business Fluctuations', in Jerzy Osiatyński (ed.) *Collected Works of Michał Kalecki. Volume I Capitalism: Business Cycles and Full Employment*. Oxford: Clarendon Press. pp. 233–318.

Kalecki, Michał 1943 [1991] 'Studies in Economic Dynamics', in Jerzy Osiatyński (ed.) *Collected Works of Michał Kalecki. Volume II Capitalism: Economic Dynamics*. Oxford: Clarendon Press. pp. 117–190.

Kalecki, Michał 1954 [1991] 'Theory of Economic Dynamics', in Jerzy Osiatyński (ed.) *Collected Works of Michał Kalecki. Volume II Capitalism: Economic Dynamics*. Oxford: Clarendon Press. pp. 205–348.

Kalecki, Michał 1963a [1993] 'Studies in Economic Dynamics', in Jerzy Osiatyński (ed.) *Collected Works of Michał Kalecki. Volume IV Socialism: Economic Growth and Efficiency of Investment*. Oxford: Clarendon Press. pp. 3–110.

Kalecki, Michał 1963 [1993] 'Problems of Financing Economic Development in a Mixed Economy', in Jerzy Osiatyński (ed.) *Collected Works of Michał Kalecki, vol. V: Developing Economies*. Oxford: Clarendon Press. pp. 23–44.

Kalecki Michał 1964 [1993] 'Observations on Social and Economic Problems of "Intermediate Regimes"', in Jerzy Osiatyński (ed.) *Collected Works of Michał Kalecki, vol. V: Developing Economies.* Oxford: Clarendon Press. pp. 6–12.

Kalecki, Michał 1990 *Collected Works of Michał Kalecki. Volume I Capitalism: Business Cycles and Full Employment,* edited by Jerzy Osiatyński. Oxford: Clarendon Press.

Kalecki, Michał 1996 *Collected Works of Michał Kalecki. Volume VI Studies in Applied Economics 1927–1941,* edited by Jerzy Osiatyński. Oxford: Clarendon Press.

Kalecki, Michał 1997 *Collected Works of Michał Kalecki. Volume VII Studies in Applied Economics 1940–1967 and Miscellanea,* edited by Jerzy Osiatyński. Oxford: Clarendon Press.

Kalecki, Michał, and Schumacher, Ernst F., 1943 [1997] 'International Clearing and long-Term Lending' in Jerzy Osiatyński (ed.) *Collected Works of Michał Kalecki. Volume VII Studies in Applied Economics 1940–1967 Miscellanea.* Oxford: Clarendon Press. pp. 226–232.

Keynes, John Maynard 1923 *A Tract on Monetary Reform.* London: Macmillan.

Keynes, John Maynard 1930 [1963] 'The Economic Possibilities for our Grandchildren', in J.M. Keynes (ed.) *Essays in Persuasion.* New York: Harcourt, Brace. pp. 358–373.

Keynes, John Maynard 1936 *The General Theory of Employment Interest and Money* London: Macmillan.

Łaski, Kazimierz 1987 'Kalecki, Michal', in J. Eatwell, M. Milgate, and P. Newman (eds.) *The New Palgrave: A Dictionary of Economics.* London: Macmillan, pp. 8–14.

Lopez, Julio and Michael Assous 2010 *Michal Kalecki.* Basingstoke: Palgrave Macmillan.

Osiatyński, Jerzy 1993 'Editorial Notes and Annexes' in Jerzy Osiatyński (ed.) *Collected Works of Michał Kalecki. Volume V Developing Countries.* Oxford: The Clarendon Press. pp. 177–237.

Osiatyński, Jerzy 2017 'Kalecki – a Pioneer of Modern Macroeconomics', *Economics and Business Review* 3(17): 3.

Peet, Richard 2009 *Unholy Trinity: The IMF, World Bank and WTO.* London: Zed Books.

Shirakawa, Masaaki 2021 'The Foreign Currency Swap Market: A Perspective from Policy-Makers', in A. Stenfors and J. Toporowski (eds.) *Unconventional Monetary Policy and Financial Stability: The Case of Japan.* Abingdon: Routledge.

Thirlwall, Anthony P. 1979 'The Balance of Payments Constraint as an Explanation of International Growth Rate Differences', *Banca Nazionale del Lavoro Quarterly Review* 32(128, March): 45–53.

Toporowski, Jan 2013 *Michał Kalecki: An Intellectual Biography. Vol. 1 Rendezvous in Cambridge 1899–1939.* Basingstoke: Palgrave Macmillan.

Toporowski, Jan 2018 *Michał Kalecki: An Intellectual Biography, Vol. 2 By Intellect Alone 1939–1970.* Basingstoke: Palgrave Macmillan.

PART I

BRETTON WOODS AND FULL EMPLOYMENT

The Kalecki Alternative

1

Michał Kalecki on International Equilibrium and Full Employment

Jerzy Osiatyński

1.1 Introduction

Michal Kalecki is to me one of the world's most original macroeconomists of the twentieth century: a man and scholar of great integrity and profound compassion for full employment and economic and social justice. I remember him as a demanding teacher but very generous with his time to his students and objective in his judgement of their work. He was also a man of a subtle sense of humour and irony, of great interest in life, and of high principle, his professional life being marked by a series of resignations from his positions in protest at violations of the standards and ethics of professional conduct.

This chapter reviews Kalecki's ideas on how to handle the problem of international equilibrium in the balance of payments while pursuing the policy of achieving and maintaining full employment. In 1943 the respective American and British plans to establish an International Stabilization Fund and an International Clearing Union (ICU) (known, after the names of their main authors, as the White and the Keynes plans respectively) were published. The essence of Kalecki's extension of Keynes's plan is examined here, as well as Kalecki's practical experience, a few years later, in the context of his supervision of the United Nations reports on full employment policies pursued by individual UN member countries and on their balance of trade positions.

Section 1.2 contains a summary of his theory of cyclical fluctuations and economic dynamics of a capitalist economy, and his theory of effective demand on which his full employment theory and its policy recommendations are founded. His discussion of political opposition to medium- and

Jerzy Osiatyński, *Michał Kalecki on International Equilibrium and Full Employment*. In: *International Equilibrium and Bretton Woods*. Edited by Jerzy Osiatyński and Jan Toporowski, Oxford University Press.
© Oxford University Press (2022). DOI: 10.1093/oso/9780192856401.003.0002

long-term maintenance of full employment is also outlined here. Important economic constraints on the policy of sustained full employment are the potential and actual disequilibria in the balance of payments. This is followed in Section 1.3 by a discussion of Kalecki's proposals on how to overcome that constraint in the context of the American and British proposals that laid foundations in 1944 for the Bretton Woods institutions. In 1946 Kalecki moved to the UN Secretariat, one of his responsibilities being the supervision of individual country reports on the implementation of their policy regarding full employment, to which they were now committed. Section 1.4 shows how Kalecki's ideas on the ways and means of keeping in check the balance of payments equilibrium while pursuing a full employment policy found reflection in those reports. Section 1.5 concludes with a discussion of the relevance of Kalecki's theory and his policy recommendations under present-day global financial capitalism.

1.2 Kalecki's Doctrine of Full Employment

Whatever economic system Kalecki studied, his main concern was full employment and the policies necessary to achieve and maintain it. An eye-witness of the 1929–33 business crises, which hit Poland exceptionally hard, the causes of that crisis, and the measures undertaken to alleviate its effects became a natural centre of his interest. The theoretical framework for this inquiry was his theory of economic dynamics and business fluctuations in a capitalist economy which in some of his papers he also called his 'economic doctrine of full employment' (see e.g. 'Political Aspects of Full Employment', Kalecki 1943 [1990]: 337–9).

Among those who know his work Kalecki is often regarded as theorizing in a closed economy. Like Keynes in his *General Theory*, Kalecki in his 1933 'Essay on the Business Cycle Theory' (1933a [1990]) and in many later publications also began research on the business cycle assuming a closed economy model, usually with no government sector. The purpose of those restrictive assumptions was to isolate and concentrate on the mechanism of business fluctuations. However, the opinion that Kalecki was a closed economy theorist is incorrect, considering that alongside his business cycle theory Kalecki was developing his theory of effective demand where he operated with an open economy model and a government sector. In fact, his very first theoretical paper 'On Activating the Balance of Trade' starts with a national output balance equation:

Social output = Final consumption + increasing property, equipment, and stocks + trade surplus

which after some manipulation he transforms (in a slightly modified form) into:

trade deficit + net income transfers from abroad + capitalization = Investments

which is a national income generation balance equation in an open economy (see Kalecki 1929 [1990]: 15–16. By 'capitalization' Kalecki meant the increase in funds saved).

Moreover, in his 1932 paper 'On the Papen Plan' Kalecki argued that 'the Papen plan, like every other plan for stimulating the business upswing, must jeopardize the currency position, unless there is a simultaneous inflow of capital from abroad'; and that 'the Papen plan differs considerably from the Nazi economic programme, which included the financing of large public works by the issuing of money, i.e. it planned the stimulation of the business upswing by means of a certain type of monetary inflation. The fight between Papen and Hitler is largely a clash between these two ideas for overcoming the crisis' (1932a [1990]: 61), which was due to the fact that Papen and Hitler each had different political followings. The underlying model is clearly one of an open economy with the government sector.

Kalecki presented a similar line of argument in several other publications of 1932–35, the most outstanding of which is his paper 'On Foreign Trade and "Domestic Exports"' (1933b [1990]) where net export and deficit financed government spending are two factors which next to private investment determine profits, aggregate demand, future investment decisions, and thereby the total volume of output and employment. And in his 1954 [1991] *Theory of Economic Dynamics* the export surplus and deficit-financed public spending are two co-determinants of his profit equation, and of his equation determining the dynamics of private investment. In an open economy model with the government sector Kalecki's argument becomes more complicated but his final conclusions are unaffected. When, in 1943, he claimed to have provided the theoretical foundations for a full employment policy he must have had in mind his theory of the business cycle and economic dynamics set in a broader context of his own version of the theory of effective demand.

What is then the core of Kalecki's 'doctrine of full employment', or indeed his version of the theory of effective demand and cyclical development of a capitalist economy?[1] The Kalecki-stylized capitalist economy operates as a rule below the full capacity use of factors of production, and the market mechanism, if left to itself, is unable to achieve and maintain full employment. The free competition assumption is rejected and oligopoly price fixing by producers of manufactured goods and of services rules. Within the 'normal' range of changes in volume of output and employment these two assumptions make the aggregate supply function run close to a horizontal line (unit prime costs constant or only slightly rising) while in the neighbourhood of full employment, it sharply rises.

The theory of income distribution according to marginal productivity is rejected and replaced by a class-conflict theory of distribution between profits and wages based on his concept of the 'degree of monopoly'. He distinguished between prices of manufactured goods and those of agricultural products and raw materials. Whereas the latter are supply determined the former are set by their producers who mark-up their unit prime costs (of labour and of raw materials and intermediate semi-products) by a gross profits margin to cover the overhead cost and earn profit. The mark-up is determined by concentration of production, by sales promotion, by the strength of trade unions, etc., i.e. by the competitive structure of the market. Considering that in the course of the business cycle the cost of labour per unit of output as a rule changes in the opposite direction to the change in the unit costs of raw materials, Kalecki found the relative shares of profits and wages in GDP to be roughly stable.[2] Given that stability, Kalecki focused on the determinants of profits and on his canonic profit equation which represents his version of effective demand theory, and on demonstrating how and why, in an open economy with a government sector, profits are determined by: (i) private investment; (ii) debt-financed government spending; and (iii) net exports, whereas changes in these components of aggregate demand determine corresponding changes in the volume of output and employment.

The key variable which decides economic dynamics and the business fluctuations of a capitalist economy is private investment which, through his profit equation and that of income distribution, is functionally linked to changes in output and employment. Investment decisions are in turn a complex function of expected profits and of the degree of employment of the existing capital stock. Why are private investments subject to cyclical fluctuations? This follows from the lag in their income generating effect and their capacity increasing effect. When an investment project is under construction, it generates additional demand and incomes which, after allowing for leakages due to private savings, taxation, and imports, create savings which in turn partially finance that project. The supply effect appears once the project is completed as it adds to production capacities and competes with plants already under operation. When the income effect dominates, it increases the present and expected profitability and encourages new investment. When the supply effect appears, it works in the opposite direction, through reducing the profitability of investment and the degree of operation of the already existing production capacities. If these two effects are left to the action of the market mechanism alone, the time lag between the income effect and the supply effect leads to cyclical fluctuations of aggregate investment, output, and employment. 'A mutual adjustment of these two effects is theoretically possible at a constant rate of investment growth and upon meeting some additional conditions, and that requires a wise macroeconomic policy' (Łaski 2019: 48). The average time lag between investment decisions and their supply effect is responsible, in Kalecki's theory, for a rather regular period of business fluctuations, whereas random shocks of normal distribution account for their neither damped nor explosive amplitude. Semi-exogenous factors, in which he included technical progress, generate in turn a positive growth trend.

As a rule, the income-generation effect of private investment is insufficient to achieving and maintaining full employment. Therefore, in the absence of an export surplus, full employment requires government intervention through either: (i) tax or other measures that stimulate private investment; (ii) debt-financed public spending on public investment or on subsidizing mass consumption;[3] or else (iii) redistribution of income to low-earning and therefore low-saving households (see Kalecki 1944 [1990]).

Absent in Kalecki's analysis is the distinction between the 'short period', in the course of which some external shocks or market imperfections may lead

---

[3] As long as the supply curve runs parallel to horizontal axes (on a diagram where costs and prices are denoted along the vertical and the volumes of output and employment along the horizontal axes), a rise in output and employment generated by deficit spending would not induce inflation. When unit prime cost and thereby the supply curve is slightly rising, the short-term quantity adjustment will nonetheless dominate the price adjustment. Only when the economy arrives close to full employment (and the supply curve shoots up) any further expansion of spending (whether public or private, domestic or foreign) will give rise to inflation, at least until capacity adjustment follows.

to underemployment of factors of production, and the 'long period' during which market mechanism would restore equilibrium at full employment. In his review of the *General Theory* Kalecki thought Keynes's treatment of factors determining the volume of investment inadequate. 'The reason for this failure lies in an approach which is basically static to a matter which is by its nature dynamic' (Kalecki 1936 [1990]: 239). This conceptual separation between the short and long run dominated mainstream economics both at Keynes's and Kalecki's times as well as at present, and has been essential for the concept of economic equilibrium. Kalecki opposed both, the distinction and the equilibrium concept thus understood. In one of his last papers on the business cycle and the trend he wrote 'the long-run trend is only a slowly changing component of a chain of short period situations; it has no independent entity' (1968 [1991]; 435). And his theory claimed the economy does not 'by nature' tend to some static or dynamic equilibrium but develops along a trajectory co-determined by private investment fluctuations and the growth factors.

This is a very crude and incomplete statement of Kalecki's doctrine of employment; in fact, of his theory of the cyclical economic dynamics of a capitalist economy. Aware of the important *practical* problems involved in implementing the policy of full employment, he believed nonetheless that his and Keynes's respective theories of effective demand solved the fundamental *theoretical* problems of achieving and maintaining full employment. The first practical problem of his concern relates to balancing the current and capital accounts of the balance of payments, and the second to mobility of labour. The former he had clearly spelled out already in the first sentence of his renowned 'Political Aspects of Full Employment' where he noted that, although in a capitalist economy full employment may be secured by a government spending programme, this can only be achieved provided that 'adequate supplies of necessary raw materials may be obtained in exchange for exports' (Kalecki 1943 [1990]: 347). His suggested solution to that problem will be discussed in Section 1.4. The question of labour mobility he handled by assuming that 'working time is variable within certain limits, which provides a sufficient elasticity in labour supply in the short period, while in the longer period one may rely on retraining of labour to restore equilibrium when the structure of demand changes' (Kalecki 1944 [1990]: 357).

First of all, however, Kalecki was concerned with political opposition to full employment. On account of three factors he believed that after WWII 'business leaders' would no longer have been able to oppose any kind of counter-cyclical government intervention and would have had to accept some kind of full employment policy. The first factor was the nearly full employment maintained during the war, the second was the development of a theoretical understanding of how a full employment policy would work, and the third was the resulting slogan which was at the time deeply rooted in the thinking of the working class: 'unemployment never again' (see Kalecki 1943 [1990]: 353). He wrote:

> Clearly, higher output and employment benefit not only workers but entrepreneurs as well, because the latter's profits rise. And the policy of full employment outlined above does not encroach upon profits because it does not involve any additional taxation. The entrepreneurs in the slump are longing for a boom; why do they not gladly accept the synthetic boom which the government is able to offer them?
>
> (Kalecki 1943 [1990]: 349)

He subdivided the reasons for that opposition into three categories of which opposition against the continued maintenance of full employment he thought most important, and this for the following reasons:

> Indeed, under a regime of permanent full employment, the 'sack' would cease to play its role as a disciplinary measure. The social position of the boss would be undermined, and the self-assurance and class-consciousness of the working class would grow. Strikes for wage increases and improvements of conditions of work would create political tension. It is true that profits would be higher under a regime of full employment than they are on the average under *laissez-faire*; and even the rise in wage rates resulting from the stronger bargaining power of the workers is less likely to reduce profits than to increase prices, and thus adversely affects only the rentier interests. But 'discipline in the factories' and 'political stability' are more appreciated by business leaders. Their class instinct tells them that lasting full employment is unsound from their point of view, and that unemployment is an integral part of the 'normal' capitalist system.
>
> (Kalecki 1943 [1990]: 351)

In conclusion, Kalecki prophetically argued that a regime of 'political business cycle' would rule. In the slump deficit-financed public investment would be undertaken to prevent large-scale unemployment. But attempts to continue that policy and maintain a high level of employment over a longer period of time would be countered by an alliance of big business and rentier interests, who 'would probably find more than one economist to declare that the situation was manifestly unsound', and would force the government to return to the orthodox policy of cutting down the budget deficit, which with time would lead to a new slump. Thus, in that regime, 'full employment would be reached only at the top of the boom, but slumps would be relatively mild and short-lived' (Kalecki 1943 [1990]: 355).

In practice, however, until the early 1970s developed capitalist economies enjoyed their 'golden age': GDP growth rates were relatively high, unemployment rates low, and the distribution of income between wages and profits relatively stable. This made Kalecki (in tandem with Tadeusz Kowalik) write their 'Observations on the "Crucial Reform"' (published posthumously in 1971 [1991]). They argued that between the beginning of World War One (WWI) and the end of WWII capitalism had gone through a deep crisis which threatened its very existence. But owing to some critical reforms it was able to survive that crisis and enjoy a rather long period of relative, though not permanent stability. However, since the mid-1970s, the situation has radically changed. Orthodox, pre-Keynesian, and pre-Kaleckian economics returned to rule university syllabuses and economic policymaking while Kalecki's concept of a 'political business cycle' became a catchword in *lingua economia*.

To what extent Kalecki's macroeconomic theory and the policy recommendations that follow from it are still relevant under the present-day, global finance-dominated, capitalist system, is an open question, much discussed by the post-Keynesians and post-Kaleckians. It will be reviewed in Section 1.5 of this chapter.

1.3 Kalecki on Full Employment and International Equilibrium

Even before WWII problems of maintaining equilibrium on the current and capital accounts of balance of payments of individual countries were already giving rise to theoretical debates and economic policy concerns. Deflationary policy was practised by governments in countries with chronic balance of payments deficits, aiming to defend their respective rates of exchange and gold reserves, lest under the gold standard their reserves were transferred to creditor countries.[4] That deflationary policy of remedying shortfalls in

---

[4] In many of his papers in the early and middle 1930s Kalecki paid great attention to balance of payments deterioration in the course of business upswing and to the consequences of protectionism. See e.g. Kalecki 1932, 1933b,1933c, 1935, all in Kalecki 1990.

external demand not by expanding domestic demand but by operating on the current account of balance of payments, led to the 1929–33 world crisis and prolonged recession, great political instability, and fascism in Europe and elsewhere, that ended with the outbreak of WWII.

Next to deflationary policies, the other form of what Joan Robinson aptly called the 'beggar-thy-neighbor policy', was depreciation of the rate of exchange of local currency which in the short run also discouraged foreign trade and increased unemployment.

> In times of general unemployment a game of beggar-my-neighbor is played between the nations, each one endeavouring to throw a larger share of the burden upon the others. As soon as one succeeds in increasing its trade balance at the expense of the rest, others retaliate, and the total volume of international trade sinks continuously, relatively to the total volume of world activity, Political, strategic and sentimental considerations add fuel to the fire, and the flames of economic nationalism blaze ever higher and higher.
>
> (Robinson 1937: 210–11)

In order to overcome those fundamental problems, the questions of the organization of post-war systems of international trade and finance were intensely debated alongside questions of war finance. In April 1943 two government plans for the post-war reconstruction of the international clearing system were announced in the USA and Great Britain.[5] On 23 May 1943 Keynes presented a revised and extended version of his plan in the British Parliament.[6] The negative consequences of stabilizing rates of exchange by means of deflationary policy, as noted by Oscar Lange, could not be avoided unless a special mechanism was established that would prevent the appearance of any significant balance of payments imbalances, and quickly correct those imbalances, should they appear. In that context, Oskar

---

[5] See *Proposals for an International Clearing Union*, CMD. 6437, London, Apr. 1943, HMSO, and the *Preliminary Draft Outline of a Proposal for an International Stabilization Plan of the United and Associated Nations made public by the Secretary of the Treasury on 7 April 1943*; US Treasury, Washington, DC 1943. Both plans were published the same day by the *New York Times*, 7 April 1943. After the names of their main authors they were called respectively Keynes's Plan and White's Plan. According to Skidelsky, (2001: 195–6) Keynes's and White's plans were drawn up in response to Germany's Funk Plan for European payments, in July 1940. For a comparison of White's and Keynes's plans see Peter Clarke's contribution, Chapter 2 in this volume.

[6] For more on Keynes's plan and the actions he took to get it implemented, see Keynes 1980: 120–3; on the affinity between Keynes's plan and that of Schacht for Germany, see Lüke 1985.

Lange highly appreciated the Keynes plan and pointed out the absence of any such mechanism in White's plan.[7]

The essence of Keynes's plan was to introduce a unit of international clearing—the bancor. It would be accepted by central banks of the British Commonwealth, the USA, and other member countries of the ICU. Its value would be expressed in terms of gold and subject to change. Member countries would fix the exchange rates of their domestic currency in relation to bancor. To settle foreign liabilities every central bank of member countries of the union would have to open an account in bancors. Balances on those accounts in principle would not be exchangeable for gold but would be carried forward. To prevent the lasting accumulation of unwanted, positive, or negative balances in bancors, should other measures prove insufficient, special measures were planned the essence of which was equalizing local currencies' exchange rates in relation to bancor (see Osiatyński, in Kalecki 1997: 523).

In August 1943 the Oxford University Institute of Statistics and Oxford University Nuffield College published a special *Supplement* to the institute's *Bulletin*. Its four papers examined Keynes's and White's plans. In the introductory chapter, F. A. Burchardt pointed out the significance of the problem and outlined the five basic criteria to be met by the new system of international trade and clearing in order to avoid the defects of the pre-war system. E. F. Schumacher in 'The New Currency Plans' put forward proposals supplementary to those of Keynes and White. In the last paper T. Balogh addressed the links between the balance of payments and full employment. Between the latter two there was a paper by Kalecki and Schumacher who pointed out that the formation of an international clearing organization would not provide the rest of the world with a sufficient supply of foreign exchange of the countries which experience notorious surpluses in their balance of payments' current accounts and rising reserves of foreign exchange (or gold). To overcome this problem, Kalecki and Schumacher proposed to establish, next to the clearing union, an affiliated investment bureau whose credit activity would assure the availability of foreign exchange of countries which experience chronic export surpluses. Thus international liquidity would be maintained in the system.[8]

---

[7] See Lange 1943 [1986]: 198–200 and Lange 1943. For a study of Keynes's plan and the proposal for a 'New International Economic System' by Kalecki and the Oxford Institute, see Lopez and Assous, 2010: 161–7.

[8] This type of arrangement was much discussed in the 1960s and known as the 'Link'. Kalecki and Schumacher were possibly first to suggest it. Their proposal was subsequently developed

In his 1946 paper Kalecki sought to combine the benefits of free international trade with those of full employment through linking the international clearing system with a system of long-term credit. Assuming that each country had to expand domestic spending until full employment was reached, permanent export surpluses would be discouraged since, with full use of capital and labour resources, such surpluses would generate increased inflation rather than expansion of output and employment. However, even if all countries were to follow the policy of full employment based on domestic expenditure, for a number of reasons (such as differences in natural endowment, in the rates of technical progress, etc.) some countries would tend to accumulate export surpluses and thereby of foreign currency reserves and gold, while others would show deficits. Moreover, the 'all-round' full employment policy based on domestic expenditure might not be followed by all countries. To overcome both those problems Kalecki introduced a scheme of international lending that would support the financing of foreign net expenditure by long-term loans. In conclusion, he wrote:

> [T]here are two alternative conditions which make certain the smooth functioning of a multilateral system of international trade: (a) that each country should maintain full employment based on domestic expenditure and on net foreign expenditure financed by international long-term lending; (b) that the level of current long-term lending from 'not fully employed countries' should be sufficiently high (this alternative may in some cases coincide with the first one [...]). If this condition is not fulfilled, 'full employment countries' may experience difficulties in balancing proceeds and outlays of foreign exchange, and this will always be the case if employment in major industrial countries is subject to significant fluctuations. If [...] these difficulties [...] are not overcome by an expansion of current international long-term lending from 'not fully employed countries,' a breakdown of pure multilateralism and its replacement by another system of international trade is unavoidable'.
>
> (Kalecki 1946 [1990]: 416)

In the course of discussions leading up to the conference at Bretton Woods, mainly between the American and British government's experts, neither Kalecki's ideas, nor other modifications of Keynes's plan suggested by the

---

by Balogh (see Balogh 1947, esp. the chapters on 'Multilateralism and Full Employment' and 'Full Employment within a Region'), and by Kalecki (1946 [1990]); cf. also Balogh 1943.

Oxford Institute were considered. When, in July 1944, the World Bank and the International Monetary Fund (IMF) were set up, they were based on the American proposal. The IMF's goal was to create a 'healthy' climate for international trade, by harmonizing its members' monetary policies, and maintaining exchange stability. In case of need the IMF could also provide temporary financial assistance to countries encountering difficulties with their balance of payments. However, maintaining full employment in tandem with external equilibrium was not included in its mandate and powers.

In March 1948 the US Congress enacted the European Recovery Program (the Marshall Plan) which was put into operation in April and continued for the next four years. Its goal was to assist the post-war reconstruction of Europe, remove trade barriers, modernize industry, and reduce the influence of Communist parties. While it temporarily alleviated the balance of payment problems in the beneficiary countries, it was not meant to solve the problem of international equilibrium combined with full employment.

1.4 Multilateralism and Full Employment: The UN Experience

With the end of 1946 Kalecki took the position of Assistant Director of the Economic Stability and Development Division in the Department of Economic Affairs of the UN Secretariat. One of the tasks of the Stability Division was to study current developments in individual economies. The section first dealt with supply shortages in the early post-war years, and the inflationary pressures caused by them, then with problems of the 1948–49 recession, and finally with inflationary and deflationary pressures related to the war in Korea. In all documents prepared by Kalecki's Economic Stability Division the problems of full employment and inflationary pressures were much discussed, as were the difficulties of post-war international equilibrium.[9]

Prior to examining how Kalecki's ideas on combining full employment with multilateral equilibria found reflection in UN publications prepared by

[9] Whereas all UN documents are published anonymously, in the name of the UN Secretary General, and are as a rule a product of teamwork; and, moreover, the studies and reports prepared by Kalecki or under his supervision do not need to accurately reflect his own views, his authorship can often be detected in the structure of the document, the method of analysis, and his specific way of argument. For instance, according to Stanisław Braun, Kalecki's friend and collaborator in the UN Stability Department, the chapter on 'Introductory Remarks on Inflationary and Deflationary Processes' in the UN Report: *Inflationary and Deflationary Tendencies, 1946-1948*, was of Kalecki's authorship alone (see UN 1949a: 5–14).

his department let us recall, however, a rather interesting incident that sheds extra light on Kalecki's approach to the problem in question in the context of the mandate of the UN and its affiliated institutions.

Following the establishment of the IMF and the International Bank for Reconstruction and Development (IBRD, or World Bank), and in line with resolutions of the 1946 Bretton Woods Conference, the Board of Executive Directors of the IBRD appointed an Advisory Council. Kalecki became one of its ten members, nominated by the United Nations. The Board expected the Advisory Council to support the policy of the bank towards developing countries by taking a resolution that would make the granting of credits by the bank depend on removal of internal controls and liberalization of foreign trade and foreign capital flows in those countries. Such a resolution would give the bank's managing directors authority to interfere in the domestic policies of the countries that applied for credits. In the course of the two meetings of the council Kalecki frustrated those expectations by pointing out that the representatives of the developed capitalist countries, who controlled the bank, recommended that the developing countries followed unrestrained *laissez faire* policy whereas they protected their own agriculture with subsidies and applied restrictions in their foreign trade and capital flows. On account of these arguments the draft resolution of the Advisory Council (prepared in advance by the Board of Directors) was rejected. Following that incident the organization of the Advisory Council was revised and Kalecki was not reappointed (see Osiatyński, in Kalecki 1997: 558–9).

The 1929–33 world crisis (the Great Depression) gave rise among other consequences to a political radicalization of the socialist parties as well as to nationalism and a strong revival of the political right, eventually leading to WWII. During the war and in the first years of the post-war reconstruction in the USA and in Europe nearly full employment prevailed.[10] These political factors (which Kalecki had already noted in his aforementioned 1944 [1990] paper on 'Three Ways to Full Employment') made the United Nations pledge its member countries and the UN-affiliated institutions to follow economic and social policies that would assist the achievement and maintainenance of full employment lest the political and social atrocities of the 1929–33 crises and mass unemployment that accompanied it reappeared.[11] By 1948

---

[10] For the 1945–47 data see UN 1947: 7, tab. 1.

[11] See Article 55 of the UN 1945 Charter which pledges the UN to promote, among other things: 'higher standards of living, full employment, and conditions of economic and social progress and development', and its Article 56 which requires that all member countries undertake the necessary actions for the achievement of the purposes set out in Article 55.

the post-war reconstruction of the US, Canada, and most West European economies was practically accomplished and inflationary pressures related to full employment of factors of production subsided. Moreover, the first symptoms of economic recession appeared in the United States (US). In fact, between June 1948 and June 1949 industrial output in the US fell by 12 per cent and unemployment increased by over 1.5 million (see UN 1949c: 8). It became doubtful whether the full employment pledge of the UN Charter might be achieved by the free play of market forces alone.

In March 1948 the UN Economic and Social Council, following the resolution adopted on 4 February 1948 by the UN Conference of Trade and Employment, endorsed the conference's opinion that the studies dealing with the achievement and maintenance of full and productive employment should be rapidly advanced, and requested the Secretary General:

(a) to arrange with Members of the United Nations [...] for the submission of information concerning action they are now taking to achieve or maintain full employment and economic stability [...], (b) to arrange with the appropriate specialized agencies for reports on plans which they have prepared and resources they will have available to assist members of the agency to prevent a decline of employment and economic activity and (c) to prepare as soon as practicable an analytical report based on information received.[12]

Implementing requests (a) and (c) of that resolution, Kalecki's Economic Stability and Development Division prepared a questionnaire which covered various aspects of the relevant economic policies and of measures actually taken or planned by individual governments in order to maintain full employment and economic stability and to prevent a decline in economic activity and employment in the future.[13] With time the annual reports increasingly reflected the waning commitment of individual responding governments to interfere with operation of the market mechanism in order

---

[12] Resolution 104 (VI), 3 March 1948, *Resolutions adopted by the Economic and Social Council during its sixth session from 2 February to 11 March 1948*, quoted after UN 1949b: 1–2.

[13] On 6 July 1948 the questionnaire was sent out to UN member countries, the associate and participating members of the regional economic commissions, and to the UN specialized agencies, the IMF and IBRD among them. By July 1949 twenty-six replies were returned and the UN report which examined them was published the same month (see UN 1949b: 5–6). The 1949 Economic and Social Council request was modified in 1950 and 1951, and by the UN General Assembly in 1952, and the questionnaires have been revised accordingly (see UN 1952: iii).

to maintain full employment. While investigating the causes of that trend may merit a separate study, let us turn here to examining the governments' and the UN specialized agencies' responses to questions on interrelations between full employment policies and the balance of payments equilibrium. In view of the pre-war experience in countering chronic disequilibria in current and capital accounts of balance of payments, the questionnaire enquired what change in policies would be undertaken by countries maintaining full employment in the face of a decline in exports, leading to balance of payment difficulties: '(i) what national measures were envisaged to handle the problem; (ii) what type of assistance would be needed of the specialized UN agencies; and (iii) what other international measures might render additional assistance' (UN 1949b: 5; parallel questions with slight modifications were included in future questionnaires, see e.g. UN 1951a: 171–2, UN 1952: 127; replies of individual countries to those questions on the whole pointed to similar measures aimed at protecting their balance of payments.[14]

In their replies, all developed market economies except the US pointed to the threat that if a single country attempted to run full employment policy in the face of deflationary pressures from abroad, due to other countries failing to maintain their domestic aggregate demand at a volume that would secure full employment, this would result in a deterioration of the balance of payments of that country. Unless it had adequate reserves of gold or foreign exchange and was prepared to draw upon them, persistent disequilibrium in its balance of payments, if not relieved by foreign lending, would seriously undermine its domestic full employment policy. One approach to deal with that problem, as put forward by Great Britain and Australia, was international action aimed at maintenance of a high and stable volume of employment and effective demand in all countries. Another suggested corrective measure was financial assistance by the IMF and the IBRD. Should appropriate assistance prove unavailable or insufficient, most responding governments contemplated import restrictions (within the limitations arising from their international commitments as member countries of the IMF and the International Trade Organization), although they were aware of

---

[14] In the UN reports mentioned above, Kalecki's approach to the full employment agenda of the surveyed countries and to linking it with maintenance of external equilibrium is seen in the structure of questionnaires, the specific questions asked, the comments on the replies of individual countries, as well as in general introductory or concluding notes therein. The questionnaires reports were much patterned along the lines of his 1944 [1990] 'Three Ways to Full Employment', his 1946 [1990] paper on multilateralism, and his many papers for the Oxford Institute on the British war economy.

retaliatory countermeasures that might well be applied by their trading partners (see UN 1949b: 21–3). No responding country in that group mentioned devaluation of their exchange rates, yet this was first to arrive.

During the 1930s the most developed market economies (including the sterling area as a whole) registered persistent deficits in their trade with the US. These were financed largely through drawings on reserves or sales of gold from current production. These methods of financing were not available in the post-war period because the deficit countries had hardly any dollar reserves and at the same time the dollar value of gold production fell, while current dollar deficits sharply increased. The dollar gap had declined by 1948 when civil production in the deficit countries returned to roughly normal and post-war emergency imports from the dollar area could be reduced. Moreover, part of the US post-war exports was financed by the European Recovery Program. The export surplus of the US declined from US$9,500 million in 1947 to US$5,500 million in 1948. However, in 1949 that gap increased again and by mid-1949 it reached US$7,000 million (annualized; see UN 1951b: 168). The 1949 dollar crisis set in and on 18 September sterling was devalued by 30.5 per cent in relation to the US dollar, giving rise to a wave of devaluations in many West European countries and in Canada (see IMF 1950: App. I).

The 1949 dollar crisis and devaluations that followed made the United Nations intensify their efforts to mitigate at least deflationary policies in future while not compromising their pledge to full employment. In October 1949 the UN Secretary General appointed a small group of experts which by the end of the year had prepared their report on *National and International Measures for Full Employment* (UN 1949c).[15] Having considered domestic policies of maintaining full employment the experts turned to international measures and they also (as Keynes and Kalecki before them) expected the two Bretton Woods institutions to take more active measures towards solving the problem of multilateral log-run balance of payments equilibrium combined with full employment. Among those measure they focused on: (i) a programme to establish a new equilibrium in international trade; (ii) stable international investment for economic development (through foreign lending programmes by governments, new functions of the IBRD, and technical assistance by the United Nations); and (iii) a plan for stabilizing world trade turnover through new functions of the IMF. In order to accommodate

---

[15] The group was chaired by E. Ronald Walker and included John Maurice Clark, Arthur Smithies, Nicolas Kaldor, and Pierre Uri.

persistent deficits in the balance of payments of countries suffering from inadequate exports to cover the import requirements of full employment policy, and thus to avoid deflationary adjustment of those countries, the experts recommended the following:

> Since the International Monetary Fund is the international institution concerned with maintaining international currency reserves, the most appropriate solution of this problem would be an arrangement whereby the Fund would act as an agent for the provision of temporary accommodation to countries confronted with a loss of monetary reserves as a result of deflationary tendencies in other countries. Under such an arrangement, any country whose external disbursements on account of imports fell as a result of a fall in internal effective demand would put at the disposal of the Fund such sums in its own currency as were necessary to make up for the deficiency; these sums would, in turn, become available for purchase by other countries against their own currencies, in proportion to the losses which they had sustained in the currency of the depositor country as a result of the fall in their exports to that country. For this process to be self-liquidating, a further provision would be required whereby the depositor country would, in some subsequent period, be able to replenish its own monetary reserves by drawing upon such other currencies as had been deposited with the Fund under the above purchasing arrangements.
>
> (UN 1949c: 63)[16]

The response of the IMF and the World Bank to those initiatives was rather adverse. Possibly less sensitive than individual governments to changing political pressures regarding maintenance of full employment after WWII, the leaderships of Bretton Woods institutions were intellectually and politically more attached to economic liberalism, free markets, and 'small government' ideology. Replying to the UN 1949b full-employment questionnaire, regarding the extent to which the IMF would be prepared to grant assistance to member countries and the resources that would be available for that purpose, the fund declared that under its statutes although it was authorized to make financial resources available to member countries and thus to assist their actions aimed at correcting maladjustments in their balance of payments 'without resorting to measures destructive of national or international

---

[16] The scheme of the IMF additional functions recommended by the experts was set out in detail (see UN 1949b: 96–9).

prosperity', the fund resources were intended primarily to relieve temporary disequilibria in the balance of payments of member countries. The fund also noted that its resources 'are not and cannot be large enough to give all its members the assurance simultaneously that in the event of a world crisis sufficient finance of the kind which they urgently need will be available to afford complete protection against balance of payments pressures'.[17] The World Bank's reply likewise stressed that its mandate basically ruled out any counter-cyclical funding.[18]

July 2019 marked the 75th anniversary of the establishment of Bretton Woods institutions. Summarizing the conclusions of the 2019 *Bretton Woods@75 Compendium*, Martin Wolf notes that in the course of those years national income per capita increased fourfold, the volume of trade increased over forty times, and the proportion of the world's population living below the extreme poverty line declined from 75 per cent in 1950 to 10 per cent in 2015 (Wolf 2019: 8). The Bretton Woods institutions had made a fair contribution to that success. However, although they were built on ideas of international cooperation for the attainment of common goals, the IMF and the IBRD, devoid of any systematic and institutionalized mechanism of restoring persistent balance of payments disequilibria, throughout their history proved unable to solve that intractable problem. In the face of mounting balance of payments disequilibria, in 1971 the regime of fixed but adjustable exchange rates collapsed, and shortly afterwards governments abandoned the goal of full employment. The IMF Special Drawing Rights system, that had been in operation since 1969 to supplement shortfalls of preferred foreign exchange reserve assets proved inadequate. Protecting national interests through a new form of 'beggar-thy-neighbor' policy by means of depressing the rates of growth of wage-rate against their rates of growth in competing countries have resulted, among other things, in intensified deflationary pressures and tendencies to economic stagnation in Europe and elsewhere.

Wolf rightly notes that the Bretton Woods system 'shaped the post-WWII era not so much because of the specific agreements reached, but because of

---

[17] Both quotes after UN 1949b: 22; for details, see also pp. 94–7.

[18] According to Toporowski, 'This echoes some early 1990s discussions as to whether the IMF could serve as a lender of last resort to the international monetary system. A conclusion was that the IMF could not take this role because it cannot "flood the international money markets with money". Only one institution can do this, and that is the US Federal Reserve. In practice this latter solution has been accepted in the FED swap arrangements with central banks such as the Bank of England, the ECB, the Bank of Japan, etc.' (personal communication with Osiatyński, 26 July 2019).

the commitment to institutional cooperation it embodied' and asks how that cooperative global economic order could be sustained. Following the focus of the *Compendium* on the international aspects of ensuring stability of that global order he shares the opinion that

> [i]t includes the management of monetary and financial systems, the future of development policy and the prospects for world trade, which were all part of the debates at and around Bretton Woods. [...] One traditional issue is the reliance on the US dollar in the global monetary system. This was unresolved at Bretton Woods, when John Maynard Keynes proposed a global currency.
>
> (Wolf, 2019: 8)

Following Jean-Claude Trichet, Wolf seems to believe that while a supranational currency remains impossible (which is right), the IMF's Special Drawing Rights system could assume the function of securing a multilateral balance of payments equilibrium. This is doubtful. It did not prevent the collapse in 1971 of the fixed exchange rate system, or many subsequent large balance of payments disequilibria. To achieve multilateral balance of payments equilibrium without resorting to deflationary policies and national protectionism—notwithstanding whether the policy of maintained full employment is actually pursued or not—requires now, as it had in the early post-war years, extra international powers and institutional capacity—the idea that lies at the root of Kalecki's 1946 paper.

The last decade saw attempts, inspired by the Keynes's plan, to solve the problem of combining improved prosperity with multilateral external equilibrium at a regional level. In 2009 the SECURE payment system was established by seven Latin American countries, and in 2012 the European Central Bank (ECB) launched its TARGET2 scheme for the Eurosystem countries.[19] While Keynes wanted the ICU to use the foreign exchange reserves of creditor countries to fund loans extended to debtor countries, the ECB may not do that. However, as noted by Chmielewski and Sławiński (2019: 58–60), while the ICU aimed at mitigating balance of payments imbalances, giving the debtor countries time to adjust their economies, the

---

[19] See e.g., Barredo-Zuriarrain and Cerezal-Callizo (2019) who note that 'to make the TARGET2 a mechanism for the progressive and symmetric adjustment of imbalances in the Eurozone, this mechanism should not coexist with other parallel systems of monetary and financial relations' and that the same applies to SUCRE (Barredo-Zuriarrain and Cerezal-Callizo (2019: 51). See also Chmielewski and Sławiński (2019).

Eurosystem through its TARGET2 scheme almost automatically restores balance of payments equilibrium, and they conclude that

> the experiences with TARGET2 indirectly confirm the superiority of Keynes' plan, which involved the establishment of a global central bank, over the White Plan which proposed to set up a stabilization fund. Had the IMF become a global central bank rather than a stabilization fund the global shortage of reserve currency in the 1950s and 1960s would have been less pronounced.
>
> (Chmielewski and Sławiński (2019: 60)

Some questions in Keynes's as well as in Kalecki and Schumacher's argument are left open.[20] Presumably for tactical reasons, Keynes did not write that, should the ICU became a true central bank, with time the source of bancor supply, next to their transfers from chronic export surplus countries would also be their emission by ICU. Keynes knew that would hardly be acceptable even among the strong supporters of his idea. For similar reasons, Kalecki and Schmacher explained how the long-term credits granted by the International Investment Board (IIB) should be booked in the respective balances of payment accounts (Kalecki 1943 [1997]: 229) but they did not say what would be the source of their financing. They might have thought that an undercapacity use of factors of production the undertaken investment projects would partly finance themselves. Moreover, for Kalecki and Schumacher the purpose of the IIB was not merely to supplement insufficient foreign currency reserves of the debtor countries, but also to provide credit lines for the IIB from which the latter would in turn grant long-term credits for those countries. Sławiński thinks Kalecki and Schumacher were aware that should they at that time explicitly write about credit lines opened by ICU for the IIB, the export surplus countries would surely reject any such plans. This would explain the euphemistic phrase ending their argument: 'Thus the International Investment Board would not have a *monopoly* of foreign lending. Its activities would be additional and supplementary to other types of long-term lending as they have existed hitherto' (Kalecki and Schumacher, ed. cit.: 231).

The TARGET2 payment system does not solve the problem of the inadequacy of foreign currency reserves which the ECB cannot create at its will.

---

[20] I am grateful to Professor Andrzej Sławiński who in a private correspondence shared with me the argument summarized in this and the next paragraphs.

Neither can it solve the problem of financing long-term investment projects undertaken by central and local governments or the corporate sector. This is the mandate of the World Bank, the European Investment Bank (EIB), and similar regional development banks and financial institutions. However, since within the Euro area the ECB grants to its branches (i.e. the member countries' central banks) the powers to provide liquidity to commercial banks (within limits), and liquid reserves of commercial banks are at the same time their Euro-denominated currency reserves, the TARGET2 system appears to be an important step towards the aims pointed out by Kalecki and Schumacher.

1.5 Kalecki's Relevance under the Present-Day Financial Capitalism

Kalecki's and Keynes's theories of effective demand and full employment were developed for economies with sovereign money, mainly domestic financing of public debt and no legal constraints on the volume of public deficit and debt in relation to gross domestic product (GDP). That macroeconomic environment corresponded to the realities of the developed capitalist economies of the early 1930s until the early 1970s. The situation has radically changed with liberalization of financial and capital flows and is much different under present-day financial capitalism. Nowadays public (as well as private) debt is financed in international capital markets, the principle of 'sound finance' is enforced by the latter and no longer by Kalecki's 'captains of industry'.[21] Moreover, when direct financing of public debt by central banks is constitutionally banned and there are firm thresholds on the ratio of public deficit or debt to GDP (also enforced by constitutions or by international treaties as for example for European Union (EU) member countries, or by similar high-powered legislation), they all limit the scope for government intervention aimed at securing aggregate demand sufficient to achieve and maintain full employment.

The second new important determinant of the present-day relevance of Kalecki's theory relates to changes in income distribution. In his canonic equations determining profits and cyclical changes of private investment, and thereby of GDP and employment, the relative shares of profits and wages are assumed constant while the propensity to save out of wages is assumed

---

[21] Except for countries whose money is used as international currency reserve (e.g., US$ or UK£ sterling) and/or whose public debt is mainly domestically financed (e.g. Japan).

to be negligible (and only taken into account starting with his *Theory of Economic Dynamics* (Kalecki 1954 [1991]: 242–5, 248–9). However, in the past half century or so relative shares of profits are rising as are savings out of high-income households. Although these changes may be accommodated within the Kaleckian theoretical framework, rising household savings have important political implications as well as economic ones.

For Kalecki, the undistributed profits of firms encourage investment decisions and facilitate their execution and in this way stimulate business expansion. Household savings, however, depress aggregate demand and thereby investment, because at any given volume of intended private investment the gap between what the business is willing to borrow over and above its retained profits and the volume of net financial assets which households plan to acquire increases. Unless this rising gap is absorbed by debt-financed government spending, or by increased demand from the rest of the world, the adjustment process that would bring realized savings to equilibrium with realized investment would be effected through a reduced volume of output and employment. However, with rising savings of high-income households there follows a change in economic policy priorities and fighting inflation becomes an important policy goal. 'The trade-off between full employment and acceptable inflation rates seems to have moved towards tolerating more unemployment, although this may change with social polarization, political radicalization and a rising tide of nationalisms across the world, all of which are correlated with unemployment and social marginalization' (Osiatyński, 2019: 315).

Third, the driving force of Schumpeterian–innovative entrepreneurs as well as of rent-seekers is earning profit. The wealth gains related to rent-seeking compete with entrepreneurially motivated investment decisions to expand fixed capital assets. With the expansion of financial capitalists compared to Schumpeterian businessmen the power of rentiers increases while entrepreneurs are also guided by the wealth effects of their financial investment, the latter becoming an important co-determinant of the course of the business cycle and economic dynamics. When both enterprise and the household sector engage in speculative gambling in global financial markets rather than in expanding capital assets, this not only adds to stagnatory pressures in the economy but, moreover, may also require a rather substantial revision of Kalecki's macroeconomic framework.[22]

---

[22] See Davis, 2016, who examines the process of financialization of the US nonfinancial corporations (NFCs) and concludes:

This brings me to the last point regarding the present-day relevance of Kalecki's theory. What kind of macroeconomic model is needed to represent the dynamics of an economy in which speculation in financial markets dominates over investing into expansion of real capital assets? To what extent are instability and business fluctuations at present of a Minskian rather than of a Kaleckian nature? In the Minskian 'financial theory of investment', the primary cause and the trigger of financial crises are breakdowns in financial markets which are next transmitted to the real sector of economy.[23] What are the key differences between Minsky's theory and Kalecki's theory of the business cycle? For Minsky waves of optimism and pessimism in financial and capital markets, caused by financing of portfolio or fixed-capital investments, result in a succession of financial crises and recoveries. Neither duration, nor amplitude of those fluctuations is clearly determined. In contrast, for Kalecki the business cycle is an inherent feature of investing in productive capital assets that takes place in the real sector of the economy. As noted in section 1.2, the primary cause of business fluctuations is the time lag between the income effect that appears in the course of investment implementation, and the supply effect which appears only once the undertaken investment is put into operation. The financing of investment is not a separate determinant of cyclical fluctuations in investment (but an appropriate monetary policy should prevent a rise in long-term interest rates lest investment decisions were impeded). For Kalecki business fluctuations and economic dynamics are embedded in the real sector of the economy.

This is not quite the world of Minsky, nor that of the present day financial capitalism [...]. Keynes and Minsky saw the primary cause of business fluctuations in the operation of financial markets [...]. It may well be, however, that under the present-day financial capitalism business fluctuations, or

'Three stylized facts are presented, one corresponding to each part of the firm's balance sheet. First, since the early 1980s NFCs are holding a growing share of, largely liquid, financial assets relative to fixed capital in their portfolios. Second, large NFCs have become increasingly leveraged, even as the majority of NFCs have deleveraged their balance sheets. Third, there has been a change in the role of equity, especially manifested in a dramatic increase in stock buybacks concentrated among large firms Together these trends point to an increasing financial orientation among US NFCs, and an increasingly complex relationship between NFCs and financial markets. Furthermore, the sectoral decomposition emphasizes systematically different trends in financial behavior by firm size, highlighting that the behavioral changes underlying the financialization of small and large firms in the post-1980 economy differ'
(Davis 2016: 137)

[23] See Minsky 1986, 1992.

rather financial crises […], are in fact determined by global financial markets and ruled by the mechanisms discussed by Minsky rather than by those of Kalecki's theory. Then the question arises of how to expand Kalecki's analytic framework in such a way that the revised Kalecki's canonic equations of the determinants of profit and of economic dynamics should still generate regular business fluctuations in the real economy and be integrated with factors responsible for the inherent (Minskian) instability of the global financial markets?

(Osiatyński 2019: 313)

What is then the answer to the question on whether full employment combined with multilateral balance of payments equilibrium is possible in the finance dominated capitalist economy of today? Apart from the need to meet the institutional and capacity requirements for solving the problem of chronic export and import imbalances in international trade discussed in Section 1.5 above, one may need a new investment decision function that would combine Kaleckian and Minskian (other?) determinants of financial and business cycles and economic dynamics. We are, I believe, still searching for a satisfactory answer to that question.

Acknowledgements

The author is grateful to Jan Toporowski for comments on and corrections to an earlier draft.

References

Balogh, Thomas 1943 'The Foreign Balance and Full Employment', *Bulletin of the Oxford Institute of Statistics* 5(Supp. 5).

Balogh, Thomas 1947 'The International Aspects of Full Employment', in *The Economics of Full Employment*. Oxford: Basil Blackwell. pp. 126–180.

Barredo-Zuriarrain, Juan and Manuel Cerezal-Callizo 2019 'Lessons from the SUCRE and TARGET2 Systems for a Sound International Monetary System in a Financialized Economy', *Journal of Post-Keynesian Economics* 42(1): 39–58.

Chmielewski, Tomasz and Andrzej Sławiński 2019 'Lessons of TARGET2 Imbalances: The Case for the ECB Being a Lender of Last Resort', *Economics and Business Review* 5(19): No. 2.

Davis, Leila E. 2016 'Identifying the 'Fnancialization' of the Nonfinancial Corporation in the U.S. Economy: A Decomposition of Firm-Level Balance Sheets', *Journal of Post-Keynesian Economics* 39(1): 115–41.

IMF (International Monetary Fund) 1950 *Annual Report of the International Monetary Fund*. Washington, DC: International Monetary Fund.

Kalecki, Michał, 1929[1990] 'On Activating the Balance of Trade' in Jerzy Osiatyński (ed.) *Collected Works of Michał Kalecki. Volume I Capitalism: Business Cycles and Full Employment*. Oxford: Clarendon Press, 1990, pp. 15–20.

Kalecki, Michał, 1932a[1990] 'On the Papen Plan' in Jerzy Osiatyński (ed.) *Collected Works of Michał Kalecki. Volume I Capitalism: Business Cycles and Full Employment*. Oxford: Clarendon Press, 1990, pp. 60–62.

Kalecki, Michał 1932 [1990] 'The Business Cycle and Inflation', in Jerzy Osiatyński (ed.) *Collected Works of Michał Kalecki. Volume I Capitalism: Business Cycles and Full Employment*. Oxford: Clarendon Press, 1990 pp. 147–155.

Kalecki, Michał 1933a [1990] 'Essay on the Business Cycle Theory', in Jerzy Osiatyński (ed.) *Collected Works of Michał Kalecki. Volume I Capitalism: Business Cycles and Full Employment*. Oxford: Clarendon Press, 1990.

Kalecki, Michał 1933b [1990] 'On Foreign Trade and "Domestic Exports"', in Jerzy Osiatyński (ed.) *Collected Works of Michał Kalecki. Volume I Capitalism: Business Cycles and Full Employment*. Oxford: Clarendon Press, 1990.

Kalecki, Michał 1933c [1990] 'Stimulating the World Business Upswing', in Jerzy Osiatyński (ed.) *Collected Works of Michał Kalecki. Volume I Capitalism: Business Cycles and Full Employment*. Oxford: Clarendon Press, 1990.

Kalecki, Michał 1935 [1990] 'The Business Upswing and the Balance of Payments', in Jerzy Osiatyński (ed.) *Collected Works of Michał Kalecki. Volume I Capitalism: Business Cycles and Full Employment*. Oxford: Clarendon Press, 1990.

Kalecki, Michał 1936 [1990] 'Some Remarks on Keynes's Theory', in Jerzy Osiatyński (ed.) *Collected Works of Michał Kalecki. Volume I Capitalism: Business Cycles and Full Employment*. Oxford: Clarendon Press, 1990.

Kalecki, Michał 1943 [1990] 'Political Aspects of Full Employment', in Jerzy Osiatyński (ed.) *Collected Works of Michał Kalecki. Volume I Capitalism: Business Cycles and Full Employment*. Oxford: Clarendon Press, 1990.

Kalecki, Michał 1944 [1990] 'Three Ways to Full Employment', in Jerzy Osiatyński (ed.) *Collected Works of Michał Kalecki. Volume I Capitalism: Business Cycles and Full Employment*. Oxford: Clarendon Press, 1990.

Kalecki, Michał 1946 [1990] 'Multilateralism and Full Employment', in Jerzy Osiatyński (ed.) *Collected Works of Michał Kalecki. Volume I Capitalism: Business Cycles and Full Employment*. Clarendon Press, 1990.

Kalecki, Michał 1990 *Collected Works of Michał Kalecki. Volume I Capitalism: Business Cycles and Full Employment*, edited by Jerzy Osiatyński. Oxford: Clarendon Press.

Kalecki, Michał 1954 [1991] Theory of Economic Dynamics: An Essay in Cyclical and Long-Run Changes in Capitalist Economy, in Jerzy Osiatyński (ed.)

Collected Works of Michał Kalecki. Volume II Capitalism: Economic Dynamics. Oxford: Clarendon Press, 1991.

Kalecki, Michał 1968 [1991] 'Trend and the Business Cycle', in Jerzy Osiatyński (ed.) *Collected Works of Michał Kalecki.Volume II Capitalism: Economic Dynamics.* Oxford: Clarendon Press, 1991.

Kalecki, Michał 1991 *Collected Works of Michał Kalecki. Volume II Capitalism: Economic Dynamics,* edited by Jerzy Osiatyński. Oxford: Clarendon Press.

Kalecki, Michał 1996 *Collected Works of Michał Kalecki. Volume VI Studies in Applied Economics 1927–1941,* edited by Jerzy Osiatyński. Oxford: Clarendon Press.

Kalecki, Michał, 1997 *Collected Works of Michał Kalecki. Volume VII Studies in Applied Economics 1940–1967 and Miscellanea,* edited by Jerzy Osiatyński. Oxford: Clarendon Press.

Kalecki, Michał, and Tadeusz Kowalik 1971 [1991] 'Observations on the "Crucial Reform"', in Jerzy Osiatyński (ed.) *Collected Works of Michał Kalecki.Volume II Capitalism: Economic Dynamics.* Oxford: Clarendon Press, 1991.

Kalecki, Michał and E. F. Schumacher 1943 [Kalecki 1997] 'International Clearing and Long-Term Lending', in Jerzy Osiatyński (ed.) *Collected Works of Michał Kalecki. Studies in Applied Economics 1927–1941.* Oxford: Clarendon Press, 1997.

Keynes, John Maynard 1980 *The Collected Writings of John Maynard Keynes, Volume XXV Activities 1940–1944 Shaping the Post-War World: The Clearing Union,* edited by Donald Moggridge. London and Cambridge: Macmillan and Cambridge University Press.

Lange, O. 1943 'Post-War Finance Plans' (sent on 16 April 1943 to the Editor of the *New York Herald Tribune*), Oskar Lange Papers, Archives of the Polish Academy of Sciences, No. III–309.

Lange, Oskar, 1943 [1986] *Dzieła tom 8 Działalność naukowa i społeczna 1904–1965* (Collected Works. Volume 8 Scientific and Social Activities 1904–1965). Warsaw: Państwowe Wydawnictwo Ekonomiczne.

Łaski, Kazimierz, 2019 *Lectures in Macroeconomics A Capitalist Economy Without Unemployment* edited by Jerzy Osiatyński and Jan Toporowski, Oxford: Oxford University Press

Lopez, Julio and Michael Assous 2010 *Michal Kalecki.* Basingstoke: Palgrave Macmillan.

Lüke, Rolf E. 1985 'The Schacht and the Keynes Plans', *Banca Nazionale del Lavoro Quarterly Review,* 152. pp. 65–76.

Minsky, Hyman P. 1992 'The Financial Instability Hypothesis'. Working Paper No. 74. Annandale-On-Hudson, NY: Levy Economics Institute of Bard College.

Minsky, Hyman P. 1986 *Stabilizing an Unstable Economy.* New Haven, CT: Yale University Press.

Osiatyński, Jerzy 2019 'Kazimierz Łaski's *Lectures in Macroeconomics* under Financial Capitalism', *European Journal of Economics and Economic Policies: Intervention.* Vol. 17, No. 3, pp. 413–417.

Robinson, Joan 1937 *Essays in the Theory of Employment*. London: Macmillan.

Skidelsky, Robert 2001 *John Maynard Keynes. Volume Three: Fighting for Freedom 1937–1946*. New York: Penguin.

UN (United Nations) 1945 *Charter of the United Nations and the Statute of the International Court of Justice*. San Francisco, CA: UN.

UN (United Nations) 1947 *Survey of Current Inflationary and Deflationary Tendencies*. Lake Success and New York, NY: UN.

UN (United Nations) 1949a *Inflationary and Deflationary Tendencies, 1946–1948*. Lake Success and New York, NY: UN.

UN (United Nations) 1949b *Maintenance of Full Employment. An Analysis of Full Employment Policies of Governments and Specialized Agencies*. Lake Success and New York, NY: UN.

UN (United Nations) 1949c *National and International Measures for Full Employment: Report by a Group of Experts Appointed by the Secretary General*. Lake Success and New York: UN.

UN (United Nations) 1951a *Problems of Unemployment and Inflation 1950–51. Analysis of Replies by Governments to a United Nations Questionnaire*. New York: UN.

UN (United Nations) 1951b *World Economic Report 1949–50*. New York: UN.

UN (United Nations) 1952 *Government Policies Concerning Unemployment, Inflation and Balance of Payments 1951–52. Analysis of replies by governments to a United Nations questionnaire*. New York: UN.

Wolf, Martin 2019 'Renewing the rules of good behavior', *Financial Times*, 11 July.

2

The Keynes Plan and the White Plan at Bretton Woods

Peter Clarke

2.1 The Wartime Context

The significance of the name 'Bretton Woods' rests on the claim that it marked a new era in international economic policy, notably through creating institutions that recast trade and currency relations. This one event was what made this small, peaceful, mountain resort town in New Hampshire famous. But what actually happened was—inevitably and crucially—an outcome of World War Two (WWII). No less than the results of the notorious meeting of the 'Big Three' at Yalta a few months later, subsequently known simply as 'Bretton Woods', depended on the current state of relations between the victorious allies. The D-Day landings in Normandy by American and British Empire forces came in June 1944, and the military outcome hung in the balance while the Bretton Woods conference deliberated during July.

In particular, a combination of undue optimism about the war in Europe and undue pessimism about the war in the Pacific theatre had important financial and economic implications for the British. The current assumption was that American support for the British war effort through Lend–Lease would continue for just a matter of weeks rather than months until German surrender—but with a further transitional period of perhaps 18 months before a Japanese surrender, giving plenty of time for these two close allies to work out their own post-war financial settlement between themselves. As things actually turned out, after a hard winter and an amazing rearguard action by the Germans, VE-Day did not arrive until May 1945; but VJ-Day then came only 3 months later, once the atomic bombs were dropped at Hiroshima and Nagasaki in August 1945. Roosevelt was now dead; his

Peter Clarke, *The Keynes Plan and the White Plan at Bretton Woods*. In: *International Equilibrium and Bretton Woods*. Edited by Jerzy Osiatyński and Jan Toporowski, Oxford University Press.
© Oxford University Press (2022). DOI: 10.1093/oso/9780192856401.003.0003

inexperienced successor President Truman ended Lend–Lease to Britain within a few days.

For the British this acute post-war crisis came more suddenly than anyone had anticipated at the time of the Bretton Woods conference. Their key advisor and negotiator on international finance, Lord Keynes, called it 'a financial Dunkirk'. He was to go to the United States in the autumn of 1945 pleading for further subventions; and what he was offered by the Americans, in the form of a huge dollar loan that was only paid off by the British Government in 2006, was hardly what had been envisaged in July 1944. Thus British ratification of the Bretton Woods agreement, notably its conditions for making sterling convertible with the dollar, now became a requisite for Britain getting the necessary dollars. The technical link was that the American loan agreement demanded that the Bretton Woods provision for sterling to become freely convertible (in practice into dollars) was now to take place on a fixed and accelerated timetable.

Even in 1944 the plain fact was that the conference was held on American soil and organized along American lines, including the participation of large numbers of lawyers. When two new institutions were set up—the International Monetary Fund (IMF) and the World Bank—the British had confidently assumed that the headquarters of one should be in London; but both were assigned to Washington, DC, where, so the British argued, they would be too much under the political influence of the US government. But that was exactly the point.

The hosts at Bretton Woods had not been the US State Department, under its Secretary of State, the ideological free trader Cordell Hull. Instead, Hull was deliberately excluded and the US Treasury had taken charge. Its secretary, Henry Morgenthau, a close confidant of Roosevelt, was given a high honorific role. But in personal terms everyone agreed that the work was dominated by two figures. One was Harry White for the US Treasury, an economist himself, very able, trusted by Morgenthau, a committed 'New Dealer' and (as we now know) a fellow traveller who was passing sensitive information to the Soviet Union (Steil 2013: 4–6). The other was John Maynard Keynes (Lord Keynes as he had become in 1942) as head of the UK delegation. His actual governmental position was almost impossible to define; he had no rank, he took no salary, he was 'just Keynes', licensed to intervene where he chose.

And, of course, he was the most famous economist in the world. He was more famous than White; indeed, White had to endure US press comment that he was in awe of Keynes. One observer at Bretton Woods said: 'The happiest moment in the life of Harry White came when he could call Keynes by his first name' (Gardner 1980: 111)—maybe. Both of them were much more famous than Kalecki, who had made highly pertinent comments on the issues at stake that are certainly still worth exploring today. But such levels of relative fame among economists did not, at the relevant time, determine the outcome of arguments about international financial policy. Nor did the long-term relevance of their arguments, not least those affecting the fate of developing countries, where we can recognize today that Kalecki had much to impart—if only the decision makers at Bretton Woods had been listening.

We need to explore the context in which a Keynes plan, and then a rival White plan, had originated from 1941 onwards; and, in particular, to understand why Keynes contrived to agree on the proposals that became the agenda for Bretton Woods in 1944. For this represented a dilution or even a betrayal of the Keynes plan in the form in which it had originally been presented and discussed. In this context, it can be seen that much in the Keynes plan that had initially attracted Kalecki's sympathetic attention in 1943 had meanwhile been subsumed or subverted within an agreed compromise that was closer to the American White plan. And the responsibility for this reorientation lay with Keynes himself, now acting not as an economist so much as an emissary of the increasingly beleaguered British government, with its dependence on American support ever more evident.

**

2.2 'Bancor' and the Gold Standard

It was as early as 1941 that Keynes first formulated his views on what he initially called an International Currency Union (CU)—a name changed in his later drafts in 1942 to International Clearing Union (ICU). The proposal in these drafts that some sort of international currency should be created—this was to be called 'bancor'—has received subsequent attention, most recently in the era of the euro when some of the issues raised about international equilibrium and the impact of making settlements between creditor countries and debtor countries were intrinsically similar.

But if we are trying to understand the significance of the Keynes plan for Bretton Woods, one significant fact to remember is that 'bancor' did not form part of the proposals put to the conference. When Keynes outlined the agenda for Bretton Woods to the House of Lords before he left for the United States in May 1944, he made light of this by saying 'there is no longer any need for a new-fangled international monetary unit. Your Lordships will remember how little any of us liked the names proposed—bancor, unitas, dolphin, bezant, daric and heaven knows what' (JMK 26: 10).[1] Bye-bye, bancor. Or as Keynes put it, 'it has been the dog that died'.

But this was not actually a laughing matter. If a new international currency was not needed, why not? Did it mean that Bretton Woods was actually a great camouflage operation for restoring the gold standard? Keynes repeatedly denied this, appealing to his own track record as a notorious critic of the gold standard—an effective rhetorical point but not surely the end of the argument.

It is an argument helpfully rehearsed and explored in the literature. The notable milestones here are the classic biography of Keynes by Roy Harrod (1951), who himself played a significant role here, and whose account is thus supplemented rather than superseded in the two massively authoritative biographical volumes by Donald Moggridge (1992) and by Robert Skidelsky (2000). Above all, documentation is supplied by Moggridge's edition of Keynes's writings on this topic (JMK 23–26), enabling us to follow the course of Keynes's own thinking from the summer of 1941, when he first broached his ideas about post-war currency policy.

Keynes's starting point was inevitably to describe and to understand the gold standard. Historically this meant that all countries using gold as the basis of their internal currencies would likewise use gold as their medium of international exchange and settlements, whether in current trade or in overseas investment. The form in which the system operated after World War One (WWI) was actually a gold exchange system since the internal currency circulating in most countries was now paper money—but ultimately guaranteed by its convertibility into gold. I shall follow Keynes in simply using the broad term 'gold standard'.

The point about the gold standard was that it was a universal system, freely operating on gold through the central banks of all countries, which regulated their own reserves of bullion via changes in interest rates. If any surplus on the balance of payments went down, the interest rate went up, and the hot money flowed in, propping up the reserves. In practice, much of this worked by anticipation—before 1914 very little gold actually moved around the world.

---

[1] *The Collected Writings of John Maynard Keynes* are referred to in this chapter as JMK followed by the volume number. The volumes referred to are listed in full in the references at the end of this chapter.

In practice too, as most economic historians put it today, it needed a hegemonic country (which would by definition be in surplus on its international transactions) to enforce what became known as 'the rules of the game'. So all animals were equal but some were more equal than others. But all were in principle open to multilateral trade, ideally on a free trade basis, though the system still worked, albeit with some distortion, even when tariffs were applied.

This system was certainly compatible with the unique ascendancy in that era of the British Empire—an imperialism of free trade, unlike the conventional association of imperialism with a closed system of tariffs that promoted and protected bilateral trade between colonies and the metropolitan country. The Bank of England held, in our eyes, remarkably low levels of actual gold reserves because it was in effect putting them to active use rather than letting the bullion stack up in its vaults. The effect was to recycle its surpluses through the banking system, financing international investment, not only in the empire but in other then underdeveloped countries like the United States in the nineteenth century. This can be called a benign aspect of the system, even in the eyes of critics like Keynes or Kalecki, who each had their own subsequent ideas about how to stimulate such recycling processes without reliance on gold.

It was after WWI that Britain, now with an adverse balance of payments, found itself unable to play such a role any more—though the political realization of this fact was delayed. Keynes had emerged as the foremost critic of British policy, notably in two episodes: the misguided attempt to put Britain back on the gold standard at the pre-1914 parity in 1925, when Winston Churchill was at the Treasury; and the equally vain attempt to defend this parity of sterling against the dollar in the world financial crisis of 1931.

Why was the gold standard not working in the inter-war years? To Keynes it now seemed obvious that the United States was the natural successor to Britain as the major creditor nation, so it ought (as we would now put it) to assume an active hegemonic role, meaning (as Keynes put it at the time) that it ought to play by the rules of the game in actively recycling its surpluses. Perhaps the American lack of an active central bank—with the Federal Reserve System in its infancy—was an unspoken issue here. The fact was that, rather than letting cheap money and inflation adjust dollar prices in the 1920s, tight monetary policy was maintained in the United States. This had an inhibiting effect upon American investment overseas, keeping the money at home, ultimately symbolized in the vast accumulation of bullion at Fort Knox, Tennessee.

The conventional American view was naturally more complacent—just as the conventional British view had been, of course, in the days of British hegemony. But it was American policy that was now likely to prevail and WWII gave the State Department under Cordell Hull great scope to apply it. In particular, two grudges against Britain loomed large. One was that Britain had manipulated its currency, especially after the 1931 crisis, by taking the pound off the gold standard, thus in effect devaluing it against the dollar and giving sterling an unfair trading advantage. This must stop, Hull insisted.

The second American grievance was that the British had likewise manipulated trade, notably with their own Empire and Commonwealth (as the self-governing dominions were now termed). In particular the Ottawa agreements of 1932, negotiated in the Canadian capital, had instituted a system of imperial preference between the different parts of the empire, not only the colonies but especially the self-governing dominions. This was actually a desperate expedient in a crisis, but the policy enjoyed strong ideological support from the Conservative Party in Britain, which had long campaigned for preferential tariffs to bind together the empire. This was a sentiment stronger at the grassroots than in the leadership, but always capable of being roused. The notion that there were immense opportunities for bilateral trade deals between Britain and the countries of white settlement in the Commonwealth remained potent, with long-lasting echoes even today.

**

2.3 The Keynes Plan Revised

To summarize: Keynes had turned against gold in the 1920s and 1930s when British experience revealed to him the iron hand within the velvet glove. Countries in deficit were *forced* to use high interest rates to bring down prices, at a domestic cost of unemployment. Countries in surplus had the *option* of lower interest rates; but might choose to use their creditor status to amass their gold in bank vaults (or at Fort Knox) rather than recycling it. Hence there was a deflationary bias in the system as a whole because in effect the rules of the game were asymmetrical, forcing policies upon deficit countries that could only result in high unemployment. It is worth noting that such an analysis had been independently formulated by Harrod since the 1930s, which helps explain his subsequent close collaboration over the Keynes plan (Pérez Caldentey 2019: 304–5).

Thus it is not surprising that Keynes's starting point in thinking about post-war currency relations was to devise a system with a mild inflationary bias, worldwide; and this was to be achieved by recasting the rules of the game so as to make the obligations symmetrical as between creditor and debtor countries. This, I suggest, reflects the essence of Keynes's outlook as a political economist. But we should never lose sight of the fact that from 1940 onwards he was also—and increasingly—the economic statesman of a country that still thought of itself as a great power but was simultaneously under constant pressure to accommodate the views and policies and interests of the United States. This was the crucial tension that in the end determined his priorities at Bretton Woods.

From early 1941 the British war effort was fundamentally dependent on external economic support from the United States in the form of Lend–Lease, famously characterized by Churchill in a speech in November 1941 as 'the most unsordid act in the whole of recorded history'. It was in this context that Keynes had been sent to Washington in the summer of 1941, staying there for three months on a rather frustrating mission to understand US policy. Keynes met Morgenthau and reported back to London in May 1941 that 'we also discussed the question of what is called here "consideration". That is to say the ultimate terms of settlement of the Lend–Lease Bill and the sort of return we are to be expected to make in respect of it' (JMK 23: 86).

This seems a very odd way of putting the matter—as though Keynes had never heard of this 'consideration' and had to explain it to his own government. It illustrates the fact that the British and the Americans were looking at Lend–Lease through different sorts of spectacles. The Churchillian rhetoric continued to insist that no 'sordid' motives should be imputed. But in American political culture, as Keynes was evidently learning, it was only natural to apply a more transactional standard, with nothing at all dishonourable about 'a deal'. Thus each party would bring something to the table. In Lend–Lease, what the United States brought was a form of aid ultimately worth many billions of dollars—so what was the quid pro quo?

When Keynes stumbled over the alien term 'consideration' in May 1941 he was embarking on a learning curve that was to shape virtually everything that he proposed in this field in the five remaining years of his life. He tried to explain some of this to the House of Lords in December 1945, faced with the final ratification of the Bretton Woods and American Loan agreements: 'How difficult it is for nations to understand one another, even when they have the advantage of a common language. How differently things appear in Washington than in London, and how easy it is to misunderstand one another's difficulties and the real purpose which lies behind each one's ways of solving them.' He drew the conclusion that it was often better to be 'more practical and more realistic—to use two favourite American expressions' in such discussions (JMK 24: 606).

I think we should remember this experience and this perception when discussing how and why Keynes's proposals were framed as they were, and how they were adapted over time. It would be too simple to suppose that there was a visionary, highly-principled Keynes plan that fell victim to the machinations of American power politics at Bretton Woods. Keynes too was playing for high stakes in both a strategic and a tactical sense, often anticipating American reactions and sensibilities before formulating and reformulating his own proposals.

The origins of the Keynes plan lie in the ICU proposals that he drafted in September 1941—*after* Lend–Lease had been implemented but *before* the 'consideration' had been legally embodied in Article VII of the formal agreement on Lend–Lease in February 1942. Article VII will resurface in this story. It specified a joint commitment to the 'elimination of all forms of discriminatory treatment in international commerce' after the war. As the Americans understood it, this ruled out imperial preference, which had obviously sanctioned 'discrimination' within the British Empire, encouraging bilateral trade deals within the British Commonwealth, notably between Britain and New Zealand, Australia, and Canada.

Bilateralism had likewise been crucial in sustaining the Nazi war economy under Hitler's Finance Minister Dr Schacht, leading to talk of a 'Schachtian system' as the basis of the famous 'New Order' for Europe in 1940 at the height of Nazi success in conquering most of Western Europe. Its essence was to channel trade via a series of bilateral arrangements whereby goods were essentially bartered, simply running up credit or deficit balances for the two governments concerned in each of their local currencies—rather than by transfers under the gold standard. It was the rejection of gold that initially attracted Keynes. Indeed in Keynes's first draft of his own plan in September 1941 he wrote: 'Dr Schacht stumbled in desperation on something new which had in it the germs of a good technical idea'—essentially, barter (JMK 25: 23).

Keynes saw little sign of any American plan at this point. A further possible option was to build on bilateral schemes, whether described in Schachtian terms or those of imperial preference. Then, almost by elimination, Keynes came to his own 'ideal scheme which would preserve the advantages of an international means of payment universally acceptable, whilst avoiding those features of the old system which did the damage' (JMK 25: 32). This is the frame for Keynes's ICU proposals, aimed at enabling countries to clear their accounts on trade on a multilateral basis, in a way functionally similar to the gold standard *when it had worked*—but now with requirements on creditor as well as debtor countries to ensure that it really would function properly. Persistent debtor countries were required to devalue their currency—no real novelty here—but persistent creditor countries were required to revalue upwards, backed by an ultimate penalty of confiscation of their excess quota by the bank.

And nobody would actually use gold in these transactions. 'The *fundamental* provision of the scheme', Keynes wrote, 'is the establishment of a Currency Union based on international bank-money, called (let us say) bancor' (JMK 25: 72, emphasis added). There was no need for subscription of the bank's capital, since it was operating within a closed system, with deposits from some members necessarily balancing overdrafts for others, but increasing international liquidity by the magic of the banking principle. The whole point, reiterated in all the early drafts, was clear: to substitute an expansionist in place of a contractionist pressure on world trade.

But in the successive redrafting, one key change was to water down the pressure on a creditor, especially with the removal of any provision for confiscation, and instead simply to rely upon revaluation measures to correct disequilibrium. The main creditor in this era, of course, was the United States; and this is not the only way that accommodation of specific American concerns and susceptibilities was built all along in to the process of drafting.

As Keynes had said at the outset (8 September 1941): 'it is with this scheme that I should approach the United States. For it is an attempt to satisfy their fundamental requirements: it would allow us to subscribe to the blessed word "discrimination"; and it is, therefore, a system in which they might be more willing to co-operate with enthusiasm' (JMK 25: 33). This comment clearly foreshadows the British signature of Article VII, the famous 'consideration' for Lend–Lease—no discrimination. Keynes's four drafts from September 1941 to March 1942 were, I suggest, already shaped by this mindset of anticipating and accommodating the American position—whatever that turned out to be. All of this was before he had seen the White plan; most of it before a White plan even existed.

**

2.4 The Two Plans and Kalecki

The origins of the White plan had come only a week after the Japanese attack on Pearl Harbor and American entry into the war in early December

1941. The instruction came from Morgenthau but the speed of White's response suggests that he already had some thoughts on post-war financial arrangements. His first draft was ready by the end of December 1941 and discussions took place within the US Treasury until May 1942. White worked deliberately without consultation with the British—indeed avoiding any appearance of such consultation. There was no 'special relationship' here. But in July 1942 a copy of the White plan was leaked to the British—by White himself, who had his own reasons for wanting Keynes to see it at this stage.

The White plan proposed a new institution called the International Stabilization Fund to deal with the international clearing of trade balances. Countries could participate by subscribing set quotas in gold—or in US dollars, which would alone be fully convertible into gold. There was a rather shadowy scheme to use a standard unit of account, to be called 'unitas', but since this was created by subscription it was only superficially an equivalent of 'bancor', created out of thin air as bank money.

In the course of 1942–43, further drafts of both plans ensued—a total of six or eight in each case. These were now competitive proposals. The United States refused to engage in bilateral talks with the British; instead, each Treasury showed its own plan to other allies, not only in Latin America but also to Russia and China on the American side, and not only to Commonwealth countries but also to European governments in exile on the British side. In the White plan, as became increasingly apparent, the link not only with gold but also with the dollar as the only currency fully convertible into gold, was fundamental.

Yet Keynes concluded, having acknowledged these differences: 'the final results can be dressed up in terms of the language and general set-up of either plan, according to taste.' The outstanding differences in his view were the provisions for exchange control, the adequacy of the quotas, and—this was new—'the workability of the proposed solution for dealing with scarce currencies' (JMK 25: 226). This 'scarce currency clause' was a late insertion into the White plan; but it became a matter of central importance for the British. The point was that only the US dollar was likely to become 'scarce' in the sense that other countries would run out of it, or find themselves unable to meet their liabilities on trade with the United States as the universally acknowledged creditor country.

But what action, then, was open to a nation in deficit with the United States? Could it, to save precious dollars, take measures to restrict its American imports? But that was surely 'discrimination'! Yet the 'scarce-currency' language that White had now introduced seemed to license such steps. This is surely why Harrod, as Keynes's close collaborator, wrote to him with some urgency in March 1943: 'The cardinal point is that the Americans offer us in this what we could never have asked of them in the negotiations *especially after signing Article VII*, namely that we (and other countries) should be allowed to discriminate against American goods if dollars are running short' (JMK 25: 227, emphasis added).

In 1943 Keynes himself was less persuaded; but Harrod was right to the extent that the tactical value of the scarce-currency clause to the British was the fact that it came as an *American* proposal—indeed one that was to give White a great deal of subsequent embarrassment when he faced persistent criticism of it from the US Congress. It survived in the Bretton Woods agreement, though in practice its objectives were generally achieved by other means.

In April 1943 a newspaper leak precipitated the publication of the Keynes plan by the British government and the White plan by the United States, provoking public debate—including astute analysis from Kalecki and his colleague Schumacher at the Oxford Institute of Statistics. Their paper, while welcoming the approach of the Keynes plan, criticized its concentration on equilibration of international transactions on current account, rather than on capital account too, which was vital for developing countries (Toporowski 2018: 130–4). One obvious response—that this was a function delegated to other agencies (which became the World Bank)—does not entirely meet this point. Indeed Keynes's own analysis of how the gold standard had functioned successfully in the late nineteenth century pointed to Britain's hegemonic role in recycling current surpluses into *investments* in countries (many of them colonies) that were relatively undeveloped. This was now past history.

For the present moment, Keynes's attention was focused elsewhere: on the need to win American support for the problems facing countries with inevitable current account deficits after the war. In a memorandum to a Treasury colleague, explicitly outlining 'the underlying tactics' in April 1943, Keynes wrote: 'The real risk is that there will be no plan at all and that Congress will run away from their own proposal. No harm, therefore, at least so it seems to me, if the Americans work up a certain amount of patriotic fervour for their own version. Much can be done in detail hereafter to improve it' (JMK 25: 242).

This was what Keynes was already prepared to concede, showing him ready to cooperate in producing an agreed synthesis as a joint Anglo-American proposal. Indeed, the difficulty here was largely tactical on the

American side too since they still wished to avoid the appearance of collusion with the British. After much shadow boxing by both parties, an agreed plan was produced as the agenda for the proposed international conference in April 1944.

For British eyes, Keynes suggested that it was little more than the Keynes plan in new clothing. True, the proposed IMF was not to be a bank but a subscribed fund. 'These two arrangements represent alternative technical set-ups, capable of performing precisely the same functions', Keynes now argued; but the fund had 'the appearance of being closer to what is already familiar' (JMK 25: 437–8). Second, in regard to his previous proposals for putting pressure on creditor as well as debtor countries: 'These have been replaced in the new proposal by a different, *but perhaps more far-reaching*, provision with the same object in view' (JMK 25: 440, emphasis added). This turned out to be the scarce currency clause, which had assumed by this point a truly heroic projected role in rescuing the new joint proposal from the disabling flaws of the gold standard—and rescuing the British post-war balance of payments too perhaps.

∗∗

2.5 Conclusions

Thus it was essentially the White plan that formed the agenda at Bretton Woods; not just 'bancor' but the Keynes plan itself was the dog that had died. The IMF and the World Bank were set up, both duly based in Washington. There was to be no new international currency, still less a system based on the creation of bank money. Instead, a gold exchange standard was established with the actual hegemony of the dollar now institutionalized; all other currencies in the system were required to become convertible with a US dollar that alone was pegged to gold. Non-discrimination in trade was, of course, a precondition of participation in this system, thus centrally enshrining the trading principle of multilateralism.

In the end, this became the key point for Keynes. He opted for the best deal he could currently get in seizing the benefits of participation in a multilateral system. 'No country has more to gain from it than ourselves,' he declared in a letter to *The Times* in May 1944. 'For it is a characteristic of our trade that our important sources of supply are not always our best customers.' He pointed to the historic role of sterling, with its general convertibility, as intrinsic to that system—what I have called the imperialism of free trade—upon which Britain's past prosperity had relied. Hence his warning: 'To adapt a famous phrase, Schachtian minds ill consort with great Empires' (JMK 26: 8–9). Now this barb was specifically aimed at Thomas Balogh, the Hungarian economist who was also a colleague of Kalecki at the Oxford Institute. Throughout the years 1944 to 1946 Balogh was active in advising those critics of Keynes's stance, drawn disparately from the left wing of the Labour Party and the right wing of the Conservative Party, who hankered after bilateral deals, either with socialist economies or within the Commonwealth. It was an unlikely political combination but one that periodically resurfaced in the politics of this period—and surely with parallels that we can see in recent British politics.

Once the issue had polarized in this way, Keynes's priority was to reconcile multilateralism with his longstanding critique of the gold standard. In these terms, a modified White plan was perhaps his best option available in rescuing multilateral trade. But it now came with a post-war version of a gold exchange standard: one that still empowered creditor nations to call the shots on how it worked. This seemed entirely natural in American eyes in the 1940s, though rather less so later, with the post-war resurgence of Germany, Japan, and then China. It was by abandoning the dollar's fixed link with gold in 1972 that the Bretton Woods institutions were enabled to survive—but still without reinventing bancor. Wider problems in addressing international disparities, which both Keynes and Kalecki had attempted to address in their own era, have been left as ongoing challenges in the very different world of today.

Acknowledgements

I gratefully acknowledge the help I received from Richard G. Lipsey, Jerzy Osiatyński, Esteban Pérez Caldentey, and Jan Toporowski.

References

Gardner, Richard N. 1980 *Sterling-Dollar Diplomacy in Current Perspective.* New York: Columbia University Press.

Harrod, Roy F. 1951 *The Life of John Maynard Keynes.* London: Macmillan.

Keynes, John Maynard 1977 (JMK 23) *The Collected Writings of John Maynard Keynes Volume XXIII Activities 1940–3: External War Finance,* edited by Elizabeth Johnson and Donald Moggridge. Cambridge: Cambridge University Press.

Keynes, John Maynard 1978 (JMK 24) *The Collected Writings of John Maynard Keynes Volume XXIV Activities 1944–6: The Transition to Peace*, edited by Elizabeth Johnson and Donald Moggridge. Cambridge: Cambridge University Press.

Keynes, John Maynard 1980a (JMK 25) *The Collected Writings of John Maynard Keynes Volume XXV Activities 1940–4 Shaping the Post-War World: The Clearing Union*, edited by Donald Moggridge. London: Macmillan and Cambridge University Press.

Keynes, John Maynard 1980b (JMK 26) *The Collected Writings of John Maynard Keynes Volume XXVI Activities 1941–6 Shaping the Post-War World: Bretton Woods and Reparations*, edited by Donald Moggridge. Cambridge: Cambridge University Press.

Moggridge, Donald E. 1992 *John Maynard Keynes: An Economist's Biography*. London: Routledge.

Pérez Caldentey, E. 2019 *Roy Harrod*. Basingstoke: Palgrave.

Skidelsky, Robert 2000 *John Maynard Keynes, Volume 3 Fighting for Britain*. London: Macmillan.

Steil, Benn 2013 *The Battle of Bretton Woods*. Princeton, NJ: Princeton University Press.

Toporowski, Jan 2018 *Michał Kalecki An Intellectual Biography, Volume 2 By Intellect Alone 1939–1970*. Basingstoke: Palgrave.

3

Kalecki and the Problem of International Money

Jan Toporowski

3.1 Introduction

This chapter presents in broad outline the elements of what may be called the 'Oxford critique' of the Bretton Woods proposals of Keynes and White, and Kalecki's proposals for overcoming what he regarded as the limitations of the two proposals. Kalecki collaborated on this with Ernst ('Fritz') Schumacher and, less formally, with Thomas Balogh, who was certainly better known as a critic of the Keynes plan. They were concerned mainly with the foreign exchange constraint on full employment that would have arisen if governments had resorted to deflationary measures to build up foreign exchange reserves, taking them out of international circulation.

3.2 The 'Oxford Critique' and Full Employment

Kalecki's thoughts on international monetary cooperation go back to his earliest, critical views on the possibilities of individual governments achieving full employment without international cooperation. In his articles for *Przegląd Socjalistyczny* (the Socialist Review) in 1932, he had alluded to the difficulties of trying to achieve and maintain full employment in an open economy. On a unilateral basis, if one government alone attempts to reflate its economy, it risks difficulties in balancing its foreign trade, as domestic demand rises faster than demand among its trading partners. These difficulties could be overcome on a multilateral basis if reflation is coordinated with other governments, in order to ensure that all imported more so that all

Jan Toporowski, *Kalecki and the Problem of International Money*. In: *International Equilibrium and Bretton Woods*. Edited by Jerzy Osiatyński and Jan Toporowski, Oxford University Press. © Oxford University Press (2022). DOI: 10.1093/oso/9780192856401.003.0004 exported more. But this would be prone to imperialist rivalry, undermining international cooperation (Toporowski 2013: 53, 2016).

These articles were only known to a small Polish audience. But the arguments around them were common in the financial and economic diplomacy of the inter-war period, where they inhibited government action to alleviate the economic depression. The failure of the London Conference in 1933 had given way to tariffs and bilateral payment agreements between governments. Financial and economic diplomacy gave way in wartime to autarky. At the start of World War Two (WWII) regulations were introduced in Britain to give the government control over foreign assets and payments. These in effect reduced international payments to bilateral clearing between the British Government and the governments of its allies and neutral states, while freezing payments to 'hostile powers'. Already in 1941, partly in response to German plans for a payments union in Europe, economists employed in the British War Cabinet were working on the question of how bilateral payments could be replaced after the war by multilateral payments, that is, payments directly between traders in different countries and in currencies that were directly convertible against each other, so that payments from one country could be used to make payments to another country. While there was general agreement that free trade was desirable, the chief economist at the British Treasury, John Maynard Keynes and his US equivalent, Harry Dexter White, wanted to establish a system of multilateral payments in which exchange rates were fixed but adjustable, although they were famously to differ on how this was to be achieved.

In April 1943, Keynes's proposals were published in London as a government White Paper, simultaneously with the publication in Washington of White's proposals.[1] The key difference between them was that Keynes wanted a clearing union with a currency, provisionally called 'bancor', issued by an international clearing bank, that would serve as the benchmark against which exchange rates would be fixed. Trade surpluses would be automatically deposited in an investment fund for on-lending to deficit countries, and interest payments, deducted from surpluses above a certain quota necessary for trade, were supposed to discourage excessive surpluses. Governments in deficit would have automatic borrowing rights, subject to similarly modest interest payments. White's proposal was much more modest in its reserve provision and international intermediation. It envisaged an exchange rate

---

[1] White Paper 1943, and Preliminary Draft Outline of a proposal for an International Stabilization Fund, Washington, DC, 1943.

stabilization fund, into which member countries would pay gold, foreign currency, and government bonds, in exchange for overdraft facilities with a right to automatic borrowing against a quota set by the deposits of the government in the fund. Above quota borrowing would require the agreement of a majority of depositors in the fund (weighted by their deposits).[2]

In May 1943, the Government of the United States started meetings, with representatives of allies and governments associated with them, to discuss and agree financial and monetary arrangements for the post-war peace, with a clear view to avoiding the financial difficulties that had exacerbated economic instability in the 1920s and 1930s. This revival of economic diplomacy and his position in Oxford gave Kalecki a chance to address a much broader audience than the readership of the academic journals and the Bulletin of the Oxford Institute of Statistics for which he was writing. But he did so from his own characteristic point of view of the international financial conditions for, and consequences of, full employment. In the summer of 1943, a special supplement of the Bulletin was prepared. An anonymous 'Editor', in his introduction to the supplement, pointed out the link between full employment and the economic efficiency of free trade. Mass unemployment was behind the political shifts to protectionism in the inter-war period, and protectionism diminished the efficiency of international trade. This gave economic and political urgency to ensuring that there was adequate liquidity in the system.

Approximately two-thirds of the supplement consisted of a long article by Ernst Schumacher summarizing the key mechanisms of the plans proposed by Keynes and White. The summary endorsed the view in both plans that free trade alone could not secure full employment. Market forces alone would not make trade balances converge on equilibrium and the absence of equilibrium would deflate demand in trade deficit countries, reinforcing a tendency towards deflation in the global economy as a whole. But Schumacher thought that both the Keynes and the White plans were inadequate to provide the liquidity necessary to maintain multilateralism. Insufficient liquidity brought with it the danger that individual governments would revert to rationing foreign exchange or bilateralism, that is, settlements between central banks on a net basis. The net basis (transferring only the foreign currency or gold equivalent to the balance between imports and exports during the settlement period) would inevitably encourage the direction of exports towards countries from which excess imports were being

---

[2] In effect, it was the US Treasury's proposals that won out at the United National Monetary and Financial Conference at Bretton Woods in July 1944.

purchased, or else limitations on those imports. In this way, bilateralism tends to undermine free trade.

According to Schumacher, although the Keynes plan offered a higher level of international reserves to support free trade, it suffered from a lack of clarity about the concept of equilibrium. 'Under the British Plan "equilibrium" is defined as the absence of bancor credits and debits.' However, this supposes that the flow of bancor credits and debits is determined by trade flows. In fact, the balance of payments consists of three parts: the balance of trade and income payments (the current account); the balance of long-term capital flows; and the balance of short-term bank transactions. These last are the bancor credits and debits. The flaw in the Keynes plan was its presumption that long-term capital flows are balanced or non-existent, so that the balance of trade and income payments is equal to the net flow of bancor credits and debits. But if there are long-term capital flows then their balance can seriously disrupt the flows of short-term bancor credits and debits (Schumacher 1943b; see also Schumacher 1943a). Keynes did indeed advocate capital controls to eliminate such disruption. But then he could not also claim, as the White Paper stated, that foreign exchange transactions can be 'carried on as freely as in the best days of the gold standard', that is, as Schumacher noted, without even having to notify the monetary authorities of the transaction.

The third paper in the supplement was jointly written by Schumacher and Kalecki. Like Schumacher's summary paper on the White and Keynes plans, the paper co-authored with Kalecki found Keynes's plan to be preferable to White's plan. But the Keynes plan would not be effective unless modified and extended. Kalecki and Schumacher started with a fundamental critique of the whole idea that the aim of international trade policy should be balanced trade:

Both the British and the American Currency Plans are based upon the idea of 'equilibrium' ... they aim at creating rules and machinery through which, after a start has been made [after the war], each country would be 'kept in balance' with the rest of the world. Neither of them succeeds in giving more than a purely formal definition of 'equilibrium', a definition which ... is not necessarily relevant. It may be questioned whether the very concept of equilibrium is sufficiently precise and significant to be introduced at this level at all. There is no merit in a general policy aiming at Current account equilibrium for all countries, because different countries are at different stages of economic development, and a regular flow of investment from the more highly developed to the more backward regions of the world may redound to benefit of all. This is implicitly recognised in both schemes, since they are both to be supplemented by proposals for an International Investment Board.[3]

Kalecki and Schumacher did not think that charging governments for surpluses deposited in the international clearing bank would provide an adequate incentive to expand domestic demand in their countries. Some governments of surplus countries may already consider their economies to be at full employment. Kalecki and Schumacher concluded that the long-term goal of current account equilibrium should be abandoned, to allow governments to pursue whatever levels of aggregate demand they may wish to have. However, this, in the view of Kalecki and Schumacher, suffers from the disadvantage that governments might in those circumstances resort to overvaluing their currencies in the foreign exchange markets in order to hold down import costs. The authors argued that therefore currency support arrangements should be differentiated, according to whether a country has a trade deficit because it is in the process of industrialization, or because there are other reasons for the deficit. They suggested an extension of the powers of the International Investment Board (IIB) at the International Clearing Union (ICU). The proceeds of the trade surpluses of the surplus countries would be deposited with the IIB. The board would direct the surpluses to industrializing countries that had used up a quarter of their quotas as loans. However, industrializing countries that went on to use up half of their quotas would be required to devalue their currency.

The direction of loans to developing countries was supposed to allow for the additional imports required for industrialization. A further twist to the scheme was recommended by Kalecki and Schumacher to reinforce equilibrating mechanisms in industrialized countries. The IIB, they suggested, should be given the power to direct the purposes to which loans may be applied, so that loans to industrializing countries would have to be spent in industrialized countries that were in trade deficit. In this way the weak equilibrating mechanism in the Keynes plan, of charging interest to deficit

---

[3] Kalecki and Schumacher 1943. Kalecki's associate from his pre-war days in Poland, Oskar Lange, was rather more sanguine about the Keynes plan, and defended it in a lengthy letter to the *New York Times* on 9 April 1943. Lange's only criticism was that the proposed method of determining the 'fundamental disequilibrium' of exchange rates by a majority vote of the board of the International Monetary Fund (IMF) offered too much scope for political manipulation. See Lange 1986: 198–200. The International Investment Board (IIB) proposal was realized at Bretton Woods in the form of the International Bank for Reconstruction and Development (IBRD), or the World Bank.

and surplus countries, would be assisted by recycling the surpluses of industrialized countries through orders for industrial equipment for developing countries from industrialized countries in deficit. Kalecki and Schumacher defended this proposed breach in 'the free play of market forces' by pointing out that White's plan had a similar suggestion to ration the exports of surplus countries. The difference between the two proposals was that White's plan 'is neither expansionist nor multi-lateral' while the scheme proposed in Oxford provided liquidity to assist current account equilibrium in industrialized countries, while at the same time facilitating the 'unbalanced equilibrium' required in developing countries (Kalecki and Schumacher 1943 [1997]).

Unlike the Keynes plan, which sought to eliminate private capital flows, but then declared that this elimination was 'not essential' to the international clearing scheme (White Paper 1943: paras 32, 33), the Kalecki/Schumacher scheme did not altogether ban private sector capital flows. Its authors argued that net foreign short-term lending in the private sector would need to be eliminated, presumably leaving scope for short-term lending stabilized on the balance sheet of the central bank. But long-term private sector or intergovernmental lending would be allowed, providing that the lender country had exhausted half of its bancor quota. In this way, governments in surplus would only be able to engage in international lending after they had committed half of their quota to trade. However, the function of the International Investment Board would be to support current account equilibrium in countries that for development purposes needed to run current account deficits and which did not wish to become indebted to other governments and private finance. To be able to do this efficiently, Kalecki and Schumacher argued that the International Investment Board and the International Clearing Union needed to be combined in one institution, rather than separating international investment from the clearing of trade payments. In effect, this would ensure that international investment targeted at deficit countries would rise with growing trade imbalances. In contrast, the Keynes plan offered limited resources to international investment, and the White plan even more modest finance.

Two other aspects of their proposal deserve note. This is the authors' dissent from the classical doctrine that the purpose of international monetary arrangements was to assure convergence on equilibrium in the current account of the balance of payments. Kalecki and Schumacher's argument, that countries in the process of industrialization require financing to be able to run trade deficits, was to become a feature of the development economics that emerged after the war, as well as Kalecki's later approach to the economics of developing countries (United Nations 1950). The other aspect of their proposal that is perhaps even more radical, and links Kalecki's pre-war ideas on full employment with his later work on multilateralism, is the idea that trade imbalances were the inevitable outcome of attempts to reach full employment by aggregate demand management. The reason for this was that capital equipment for industrial production was not distributed among countries in such a way as to secure trade balance with full employment. The condition for full employment with trade balance was investment in productive capacity in the developing countries. The neoclassical view that prices, including exchange rates, could adjust the demand of the fully employed and their families to the resources available through balanced trade was placing demands on market mechanisms that those mechanisms could not deliver (cf. Samuelson 1964).

3.3 Support from Balogh

The final paper in the supplement was by the Hungarian economist Thomas Balogh, who was at that time a lecturer at Balliol College. Balogh had been one of the earliest critics of the Keynes plan. In his paper, entitled 'The Foreign Balance and Full Employment' (1943), he examined some of the difficulties that might be envisaged in implementing the Schumacher/Kalecki plan. His endorsement of that plan clearly suggests that the plan was a common view of the authors contributing to the supplement, if not the whole Bulletin and the Joint Committee of Nuffield College, which had worked with the Institute on that supplement. If so, then it is an extraordinary achievement by Kalecki and Schumacher, who had a mere three months to come up with a consensus on the complexities of the Keynes and White plans that would satisfy them all.

Balogh reiterated their common view that market forces would tend to work in deflationary ways in the international economy. They would be overcome by the Schumacher/Kalecki scheme for generating and financing exports of capital equipment to developing countries. One problem that he foresaw was that a requirement to use development loans to buy from mature economies in trade deficit might end up with the developing countries buying at a higher cost than they might have been able to buy from surplus countries. Balogh's answer to this was to argue for subsidies to make the cost of industrial equipment exported by deficit countries equal to that of surplus countries. He dismissed the idea that currency devaluation could do the job better, since exchange rate devaluation was a general subsidy from the domestic market to export markets, while targeted subsidies were likely to be less costly. Among the counter-arguments to this, the possibility of retaliation was less likely if all economies were enjoying high employment. The charge that subsidies might constitute 'dumping' could just as easily be levelled against currency devaluation or policies of wage reduction. In any case, subsidies would be superior to bilateral clearing agreements, which often resulted in the exchange of goods for which there was not much of a market in either country.

Finally, Balogh considered whether the scheme put forward by Kalecki and Schumacher would work equally well if adopted by a smaller group of countries instead of the whole world. In his view, such a partial scheme would work less well, because its member governments would need to take measures to counteract the effects of business cycles in countries outside the scheme and this might involve quotas for trade with countries outside the bloc. The effect of such a reduced area of the scheme would therefore depend on the degree of self-sufficiency of the bloc: in a large, self-sufficient bloc like the sterling area the loss of labour productivity due to the reduced, in relation to the world economy, scope for the international division of labour would likely be small (Balogh 1943). Balogh's suggestion arguably lays out the elements of an 'optimal' currency area, although he did not put it quite like this, some eighteen years before Robert Mundell presented his proposal based on adjustments to equilibrium in the markets for labour or foreign exchange.

3.4 The Critique Extended

In April 1944, the British Government published a White Paper, presenting the outcome of the earlier negotiations between Keynes and White on the proposed International Monetary Fund. The government still had strong reservations about the proposed fund. Chief among them was the reduction in the fund's resources in relation to the proposal in the Keynes plan, and the realization of the international investment facility as an International Bank for Reconstruction and Development, which was clearly not going to direct its resources to Great Britain, whose reconstruction and development needs were nugatory by comparison with the colonies, developing countries, and countries on the mainland of Europe. The British negotiators had therefore agreed to a reduction in the loan capacity of the Fund (White Paper 1944). Schumacher and Balogh wrote an extended comment on the White Paper for the Bulletin. They objected to the inadequate resources of the IMF, and the requirements imposed on its members. Among those requirements were the obligations to maintain free trade in accordance with criteria laid down by the fund, rather than their development needs, and to seek balanced trade which, in Schumacher and Balogh's view, could only be deflationary. They commended the Kalecki/Schumacher plan as a more effective way of avoiding deflation and offering a more discriminating way of securing trade equilibrium (Schumacher and Balogh 1944).

In May 1944 Balogh was active in London, writing to *The Times* and briefing parliamentarians on the schemes being prepared for the Bretton Woods Conference. He reiterated the arguments about the inadequacy of international reserves. But he now laid greater emphasis on the damage that would be done if the sterling area were dismantled in favour of a multilateral system with inadequate reserves. Keynes, therefore, preoccupied with his preparations for the Bretton Woods Conference in July 1944, could not have been unaware of the criticisms emanating from Oxford of his plans and agreements for the new international economic order.

Balogh summarized his views in a chapter on international trade policy in a volume published by the Oxford Institute of Statistics in 1944 entitled 'The Economics of Full Employment'. Here Balogh reiterated his criticisms of the Keynes plan for its failure to take into account the impact on trade imbalances and international monetary equilibrium of deflationary policies abroad. In a letter of the 30 December 1944 to Kalecki, complimenting him on 'The Economics of Full Employment', Keynes took issue with the section in the volume on international aspects. '[T]he section on International Aspects ... seems to me a frightful muddle, which leaves the reader more in a fog and stupider than when he began. It does not even make a beginning at the basic analysis needed to tackle this rather difficult and intractable problem.' Keynes seems to have had some difficulties himself in identifying Balogh's muddle: 'I wish I had time to think it properly through myself. It is not so difficult that it is impossible to write sense about it.' Balogh had, in Keynes's view, misquoted his speech in the House of Lords. 'What is happening to Balogh? He has done some excellent stuff in the past, but much of what I have seen of late strikes me as extremely confused' (Keynes 1980: 381).

Joan Robinson was less deprecating. Her review of the book devotes almost as much space to the section in the book on 'International Aspects' as it does to Kalecki's 'Three Ways to Full Employment'. She outlined the problem of the deflationary bias in international trade, as governments sought to bring their foreign trade balance into equilibrium, and the danger that this might lead to autarky. Her review concluded with a discussion of Balogh's suggestion that a smaller group of countries committed to full employment may form a bloc in which they would give each other preference for the purposes of their imports. 'This amounts to something like making the scarce-currency clause of the Bretton Woods proposals permanent. An adequate discussion of this scheme, which raises wide issues of international policy as well as detailed questions of the technique for planning trade in a mainly private-enterprise system, requires a volume to itself.'[4]

Joan Robinson put her finger on the problem. There is little evidence that any of the policymakers or negotiators with the United States Government were reading the analysis of international trade and finance that was coming out of Oxford. Keynes himself, as he indicated, knew only of Balogh's lobbying against the final Bretton Woods proposals, and had read only Balogh's account in the volume on 'The Economics of Full Employment'. Kalecki and Schumacher's attempt to integrate the developing countries into a supportive global financial system would have to wait for a further decade before poorer countries disadvantaged in international trade found their voice in the counsels of the United Nations.

3.5 The Full Employment Conditions

With the end of hostilities in Europe, under the tutelage of the undercapitalized International Monetary Fund (IMF), the term multilateralism came to mean the free exchange of currencies for each other, rather than the free trade that this exchange was supposed to support. Kalecki retained the view that it was this latter free trade that was important for full employment, and that inadequate monetary and financial arrangements would inhibit free trade as much as they would constrain employment. In 1946, working at the International Labour Office, Kalecki returned to the question of full employment in an open economy in his article 'Multilateralism and Full Employment'.

The article starts by pointing out that the new IMF, the IBRD, and the US loan to the UK 'aim at establishing a workable system of multilateral international trade ... the principle of multilateralism requires that each country should be guided in its purchases in other countries by the price and quality

---

[4] Robinson 1945 [1966]. The 'scarce currency' clause was an arrangement introduced by the American government allowing governments to discriminate in foreign trade against countries with persistent trade surpluses. See Kahn 'Historical Origins of the International Monetary Fund' 1976: 16–19.

of goods without taking into consideration whether the supplying countries are or are not buyers of the produce of the country in question' (Kalecki 1946 [1990]). The question to which Kalecki returned was whether countries seeking to maintain full employment would be able, under a multilateral system, to export sufficiently to pay for the amount of imports that they would have with full employment. If this could not be achieved under multilateralism, then the governments of countries trying to maintain full employment might decide that they can

> achieve more security in [their] foreign trade by concluding a series of bilateral agreements with other countries' directing import and export trade to those countries. Alternatively, a group of such countries may enter into a regional bloc, in which multilateralism operates for trade within the bloc, and proceeds of exports outside the bloc are pooled and rationed among the members of the bloc. (Kalecki 1946)

In general Kalecki was less defensive about the sterling area than was Balogh. Kalecki thought that world multilateralism was more efficient than bilateralism or regional blocs, and it would not 'raise the political issues which may be involved in the formation of regional blocks. It is therefore superior to other systems provided it is workable, i.e., provided that it is operated under conditions of such a kind that no difficulties in balancing imports of goods and services with exports arise for full-employment countries'. Kalecki therefore proposed to analyse the conditions under which full employment could be achieved and maintained in a multilateral system of international trade. Kalecki's paper not only laid down the conditions for full employment under what is commonly regarded as 'free trade'. He also showed that this requires quite restrictive conditions of international credit and debt (Kalecki 1946).

The key problem arises because in a situation of full employment in all countries, some would have trade surpluses, and some would have trade deficits. The surplus countries would continuously accumulate gold and foreign currency reserves. The deficit countries would be faced with a continuously deteriorating foreign exchange position. A condition for multilateralism to work well would be if governments in all surplus countries managed domestic demand in such a way as to eliminate all trade surpluses. In other words, full employment must not be based on a trade surplus.

However, this situation would work only if all countries maintained full employment. If employment fluctuates in some countries, then this would cause problems in balancing foreign trade: countries where employment falls short of full employment will in effect be reducing the exports of other countries, and this will transmit economic contraction to other countries. Import duties would mean the failure of multilateralism, and devaluation might increase the value of exports in domestic currency, but would be unlikely to generate additional foreign exchange. Exercising the 'scarce currency' clause of the IMF agreement, allowing discrimination against the exports of countries running persistent trade surpluses, would in effect mean a suspension of full multilateralism, and a move towards a regional bloc of the countries whose currencies are not 'scarce' (because they are in trade deficit).

The situation was modified if countries with less than full employment gave long-term loans in their currency to full employment countries. The condition for stable full employment then becomes one where 'all countries maintain full employment based on domestic expenditure and on foreign net expenditure financed by long-term loans. Thus, each country must maintain such a domestic expenditure that this expenditure plus export surplus financed by foreign lending (or minus export deficit financed by foreign borrowing) is adequate to assure full employment'. However, the difficulty with this solution is that the terms on which long-term international lending is offered may arouse a reluctance on the part of lenders and borrowers to expand international lending up to the scale necessary to overcome the difficulties with multilateralism. 'The higher, on average, and the more stable the employment in not fully employed countries and the greater their propensity to import ... the greater the chance that the achievable level of international long-term lending will be adequate for the solution of the problem.' (Kalecki 1946)

> It follows ... that there are two alternative conditions which ensure the smooth functioning of the multilateral system of international trade: (i) that each country should maintain full employment based on domestic expenditure, and on net foreign expenditure financed by international long-term lending; (ii) that the level of current long-term lending from not fully employed countries should be sufficiently high ... ... An ideal basis of multilateralism, however, will be the maintenance throughout the world of a volume of domestic expenditure which, in combination with foreign net investment financed by long-term loans, is adequate for securing full employment. (Kalecki 1946)

Failing this, Kalecki believed, countries would have difficulties in balancing their inflows and outflows of foreign exchange. This will commonly happen if employment fluctuates in the major industrial countries. If long-term international lending does not expand to overcome these difficulties, then multilateralism will break down and be replaced by a different system of international trade.

3.6 Conclusion

Kalecki's modest but substantial writings on international monetary arrangements embraced free trade as a condition for international exchange arrangements to allow the achievement of full employment in an efficient way. However, free trade had to be supported by a sufficient international liquidity backed by long-term loans to finance the investment needed to obtain full employment. Kalecki highlighted these issues in the 'Oxford critique' of Bretton Woods. However, the conference was driven by politics rather than by the views of its critics. The failure to address those criticisms led the Bretton Woods into the monetary instability and debt crises that continue to afflict the international economy.

Acknowledgements

This chapter draws on its author's biography of Kalecki (Toporowski 2018). The author is grateful to Jerzy Osiatyński for comments on and corrections to an earlier draft.

References

Balogh, Thomas 1943 'The Foreign Balance and Full Employment', *Bulletin of the Oxford University Institute of Economics and Statistics* 5(Supp. 5, 7 August): 33–9.
Balogh, Thomas 1944 'The International Aspects of Full Employment' in *The Economics of Full Employment* Six Studies in Applied Economics prepared at the Oxford Institute of Statistics Oxford: Basil Blackwell pp. 126–180.
Kahn, Richard F. 1976 'Historical Origins of the International Monetary Fund' in A. P. Thirlwall (ed.) *Keynes and International Monetary Relations: The Second Keynes Seminar Held at the University of Kent at Canterbury*. Basingstoke: Macmillan. pp. 3–35.

Kalecki, Michał 1932 [1990] 'Is a "Capitalist" Overcoming of the Crisis Possible?' in Jerzy Osiatyński (ed.) *Collected Works of Michał Kalecki Volume I Capitalism: Business Cycles and Full Employment*. Oxford: Clarendon Press. pp. 48–53.

Kalecki, Michał 1946 [1990] 'Multilateralism and Full Employment', *Canadian Journal of Economics and Political Science* 12(3): 322–7, in Jerzy Osiatyński (ed.) *Collected Works of Michał Kalecki Volume I Capitalism: Business Cycles and Full Employment*. Oxford: Clarendon Press. pp. 409–416.

Kalecki, Michał and Ernst F. Schumacher 1943 [1997] 'International Clearing and Long-Term Lending', *Bulletin of the Oxford University Institute of Economics and Statistics* 5(Supp 5, 7 August): 29–33, in Jerzy Osiatyński (ed.) *Collected Works of Michał Kalecki Volume VII Studies in Applied Economics 1940–1967 Miscellanea*. Oxford: Clarendon Press, pp. 226–232.

Keynes, John Maynard 1980 *The Collected Writings of John Maynard Keynes Volume XXVII Activities 1940–1946 Shaping the Post-War World Employment and Commodities*, edited by D.E. Moggridge. London and Cambridge: Macmillan and Cambridge University Press.

Lange, Oskar 1986 *Dzieła tom 8 działalność naukowa i społeczna* (Collected Works Volume 8 Scientific and Social Activities). Warsaw: Państwowe Wydawnictwo Naukowe.

Robinson, Joan V. 1945 [1966] 'Review of The Economics of Full Employment', *The Economics Journal* April, reprinted in *Collected Economic Papers Volume One*. Oxford: Basil Blackwell, pp. 99–104.

Samuelson, Paul A. 1964 'Theoretical Notes on Trade Problems', *Review of Economics and Statistics* 46(2): 145–54.

Schumacher, Ernst F. 1943a 'Multilateral Clearing', *Economica* New Series 10(38, May): 150–65.

Schumacher, Ernst F. 1943b 'The New Currency Plans', *Bulletin of the Oxford University Institute of Economics and Statistics* 5(Supp. 5, August 7): 8–29.

Schumacher, Ernst F. and Balogh, Thomas 1944 'An International Monetary Fund', *Bulletin of the Oxford University Institute of Economics and Statistics* 6(6, 29 April): 81–93.

Toporowski, Jan 2013 *Michał Kalecki An Intellectual Biography Volume I Rendezvous in Cambridge 1899–1939*. Basingstoke: Palgrave.

Toporowski, Jan 2016 'Multilateralism and Military Keynesianism: Completing the Analysis', *Journal of Post-Keynesian Economics* 39(4): 437–43.

Toporowski, Jan 2018 *Michał Kalecki: An Intellectual Biography Volume II By Intellect Alone 1939–1970*. Basingstoke: Palgrave.

United Nations 1950 'Growth, Disequilibrium and Disparities: Interpretation of the Process of Economic Development', in *Economic Survey of Latin America 1949*. New York: United Nations. pp. 3–85.

White Paper 1943 *Proposals for an International Clearing Union*. Cmd 6437. London: HM Stationery Office.

White Paper 1944 *Joint Statement by Experts on the Establishment of an International Monetary Fund*. Cmd 6519. London: HM Stationery Office.

4

Prebisch's Critique of Bretton Woods Plans

Its Relation to Kalecki's and Williams' Ideas

Esteban Pérez Caldentey and Matías Vernengo

4.1 Introduction

The name and work of Raúl Prebisch (1901–86) are often associated with the problem of long-term economic development in Latin America. Of particular relevance are his contributions, both theoretically and empirically, to the process of industrialization of Latin America, which he developed from 1949 onwards, during his tenure as the second Executive Secretary of the Economic Commission for Latin America and the Caribbean (ECLAC). These views are encapsulated in his text *The Economic Development of Latin America and Some of its Main Problems*, known as the 'Latin American Manifesto' which provided the basis for the work undertaken by ECLAC until the end of Prebisch's term in 1963.

Less well known and explored is the stage of Prebisch's thinking, prior to the publication of the manifesto, which he devoted to the study and analysis of the economic cycle and economic dynamics. He also focused on the monetary and financial problems of the countries of the periphery in relation to those of the centre. This led him to analyse and address the shortcomings of the post-WWII monetary plans of John Maynard Keynes (1883–1946) and Harry Dexter White (1892–1948). Prebisch thought that business cycle fluctuations in the periphery had their origin in external factors and, more precisely, in the domestic policies adopted in the cyclical centre that he saw as shifting from the United Kingdom (UK) to the United States (US). The effects of business cycles were disruptive to the process of economic

Esteban Pérez Caldentey and Matías Vernengo, *Prebisch's Critique of Bretton Woods Plans*. In: *International Equilibrium and Bretton Woods*. Edited by Jerzy Osiatyński and Jan Toporowski, Oxford University Press.
© Oxford University Press (2022). DOI: 10.1093/oso/9780192856401.003.0005

development as these could lead to significant contractions in economic activity and employment, as exemplified by the Great Depression.

Influenced by his experience as first manager of the Central Bank of the Argentine Republic between 1935 and 1943, Prebisch developed the guidelines of an autonomous national monetary policy that consisted of promoting the full utilization of resources while isolating the domestic economy from the fluctuations of the external business cycle. According to Prebisch's proposal monetary and fiscal policies were tasked with the full employment of resources. These were applied within a monetary circuit controlled in its connections with the rest of the world through the mechanism of import exchange controls. Exchange controls were the most innovative feature of Prebisch's monetary policy proposal. The regime of exchange controls was based on a hierarchy of imports that identified those that were essential to the workings of the economy and as a result should be isolated from business cycle fluctuations.

Prebisch's observations on Keynes's International Clearing Union (ICU) and White's Stabilization Fund focused on their de facto applicability, and on the degree to which these were compatible with his national autonomous monetary proposal. Prebisch praised certain aspects of the plans, such as their counter-cyclicality. He also commended Keynes's use of the banking principle as the basis for the clearing union. At the same time, Prebisch believed that the plans suffered from fundamental weaknesses which would prevent them from achieving their objective – international equilibrium in the balance of payments within an expansionary context.

Prebisch argued that the plans, and more specifically Keynes's plan, instituted an automatic mechanism that would prevent achieving full employment in the cyclical centre (i.e the US) whose growth was the basis of world economic expansion. More importantly, the international monetary plans ignored the fact that the world comprised a set of heterogeneous countries with different levels of development. As a result, economic and monetary phenomena could not be viewed through the same lens and countries could not be subject to complying with the same norms in monetary policy. Prebisch argued that countries in the periphery should have greater latitude to pursue full employment, and especially to mitigate the domestic impact of external fluctuations. This involved granting greater policy autonomy in the management of exchange rates, which was limited by international monetary plans. Prebisch ultimately thought that the John H. Williams 'key currency' proposal provided a more effective and realistic approach to achieving international equilibrium.

Prebisch's concerns regarding the country homogeneity assumption in Keynes's and White's proposals were also voiced by Michal Kalecki. Kalecki's recognition that countries were at different stages of development led him to criticize the current account equilibrium norm as the basis of the American and the British plans, as it would exert a recessionary bias to the world economy. He proposed replacing it with the concept of unbalanced equilibrium. The latter would combine balancing trade with lending through an investment agency for production purposes. Kalecki adopted a threefold classification of countries: the surplus countries, the deficit countries whose imbalances responded to needs of industrialization and reconstruction, and the deficit countries whose imbalances responded to other factors. Following the same line of thought as Prebisch, Kalecki also contemplated the possibility of using exchange controls in deficit countries to change the composition of imports in order to respond to their development needs.

This chapter is divided into four sections. Section 4.2 explains Prebisch's proposal for a national autonomous monetary policy, and his dismissal from the Central Bank of Argentina (BCRA in Spanish) just as the new international monetary plans were being developed. The Section 4.3 centres on Prebisch's critique of Keynes's and White's international monetary plans. Section 4.4 focuses on Prebisch's preferred option, Williams's 'key currency proposal', and highlights the existing similarities between Kalecki's views on the international monetary plans and the changes needed to transform these into a workable alternative with those by Prebisch. A short section concludes.

4.2 Prebisch as an Outsider

At the time the international monetary plans of Keynes and White were being developed, Prebisch was mainly concerned with an autonomous monetary policy proposal for peripheral countries, with an obvious focus on Argentina. As a result, by the time he got the plans and analysed their proposals his main preoccupation was with their compatibility with his autonomous policy proposal (Prebisch 1944a [1991]: 189–90).[1] During his

---

[1] Prebisch's writings on the international monetary plans are contained in the following works: (i) Money and Business Cycles in Argentina (1943), Volume II (Chapter II, International Monetary Problems, p. 184; Chapter VII, International Monetary Plans, pp. 236–65) This is an unpublished work. Chapter VII is reproduced in part in Vol. IV, pp. 94–112); (ii) 'Observations on International Monetary Plans', *El Trimestre Económico*, 1944, July–September, pp. 185–208,

tenure as general manager, effectively in charge of the BCRA, which started with its creation in 1935, Prebisch arrived at the conclusion that the policy objectives of central banks should expand beyond the traditional ones limited to mitigating the up and down phases of the business cycle in order to ensure their orderly occurrence and maintain the stability of money. He became aware that the central bank had a double objective – price and output stability – and that protecting the balance of payments position was central for both.

To this end he proposed the use of exchange controls which would ensure that any attempt to expand aggregate demand would not spill over to imports, thus ensuring that its effect was mainly felt in the domestic economy while at the same avoiding balance of payments disequilibrium. White also proposed the use of exchange controls in 1942 during a US Federal Reserve Mission to Cuba (Board of the Governors of the Federal Reserve, August 1942). For his part Keynes argued in favour of capital controls. The most important reason for establishing capital controls for Keynes was to maintain the freedom to vary the domestic interest rate to respond to a country's internal economic conditions (Keynes 1980a: 149, 275).

Prebisch leaned further towards advocating the full employment of resources at the domestic level while insulating the economy from external shocks, as WWII compromised Argentina's balance of payments position in 1941 due to the loss of its export markets and as the fear of general economic prostration (Prebisch 1945 [1993]: 156–7) set in.[2] The force of events led Prebisch to devise a nationally autonomous monetary policy with the aim of providing a more stable level of economic activity, reducing vulnerability to external shocks, and ensuring the most favourable conditions to

and Chapter 105 of his collected works Vol. III, Monetary Policy and International Monetary Plans 1991 (1944), pp.189–206) which is a revised version of the first article cited; and (iii) The Gold Standard and the Economic Vulnerability of Our Countries Mexico, 27 March 1944, reproduced in Vol. III, pp. 228–48.

[2] Following this line of thought the Argentine government devised a counter-cyclical action termed National Recovery Plan, also known as the Pinedo Plan, after Federico Pinedo, a former finance minister who had been central in Prebisch's political rise, even though Prebisch was the main architect of the plan. The plan contemplated an expansionary monetary policy coupled with exchange rate controls (Dosman 2008: 124–6). More specifically, the plan sought to purchase agricultural surpluses to avoid price declines, increase construction activity, and promote the finance of industrial development. Within the logic of the plan, fiscal policy played mainly a supporting role by creating the required conditions, incentives, and space for private activity to flourish. The Pinedo Plan was never implemented, and exchange controls were not applied. The force of political and external events, particularly the war effort of the United States which led to an increase in internal demand and imports, superseded it (Prebisch 1944b [1991]: 110–12, 1945 [1993]: 160). See also Llach (1984).

fulfil the growth potential of the economy. This monetary policy consisted, on the one hand, in ensuring the provision of sufficient purchasing power through the extension of domestic credit to offset the impact of a fall in exports or decline in foreign financial flows on the economy. On the other hand, it contemplated the application of exchange controls to ensure that the expansion of credit would not lead to disequilibrium in the balance of payments.

Exchange controls also mitigated the potential effects of exchange rate depreciation which included a rise in the price of imported goods and higher prices, with extraordinary benefits accruing to some sectors of the economy, and the 'protection without discrimination of the national industry' (Prebisch 1944c [1991]: 126–7). In practice the scheme of exchange control aimed to administer the level and composition of the demand for imports, as these moved in tandem with the business cycle and were outside the control of the national authorities of the periphery. Prebisch viewed the business cycle as a phenomenon initiated by the economies of the centre to which the peripheral countries had to adapt. The dynamic centre in peripheral economies was external, and that would eventually lead to the notion that it had to move internally through a process of industrialization. The proposal sought to differentiate between the categories of imports that should adapt to the business cycle from those that should be isolated from business cycle fluctuations. To this end, the government would need to establish a hierarchical order of the different import categories and, according to the circumstances, would have to prioritize the imports most needed to fulfil essential needs and carry out production.[3]

By the time Prebisch's tenure at the BCRA was terminated in 1943, he was in possession of all the necessary elements to formulate a new view of monetary policy. These were contained in unfinished form in his book proposal *Money and Economic Activity* on which he began working in 1943. In that book, he argued that monetary and financial policy should have three fundamental aims: (i) to attenuate the incidences of the abrupt changes in harvest conditions and the fluctuations and external contingencies; (ii) to create the monetary conditions that stimulate the development and maintenance of full employment of the working force; (iii) to foster and support

---

[3] The exchange control scheme sought to control imports by varying the exchange rate rather than by quantitative controls which Prebisch thought to be too complicated to implement as well as economically inefficient. The exchange control scheme would be implemented through a process of auctions. Prebisch's exchange control proposal was praised by a number of economists including Harberler (1947: 92, n. 12), Nurske (1944), and Triffin (1944).

the highest possible rate of growth of economic activity. This new view of monetary policy from the periphery provided the framework within which to analyse and critique Keynes's and White's international monetary plans.

If by this time Prebisch was an outsider in his native Argentina, and was forced to find work as a 'Money Doctor' abroad,[4] for example in the Federal Reserve Monetary Missions to Paraguay and Santo Domingo under the lead of Robert Triffin[5] (Pérez Caldentey and Vernengo 2019), the circumstances made him an outsider too when it came to discussions about the reorganization of the international monetary system – not only because he was excluded from policymaking circles in Argentina, but also because the country itself was boycotted. While Latin America had broad and important participation in the initial negotiations that led to the Bretton Woods agreements, as well as in the 1944 Bretton Woods conference, Argentina was increasingly excluded from the orbit of influence of the US despite Roosevelt's supportive policy towards Latin America. Under Roosevelt's leadership, the US engaged in a more collaborative and development friendly agenda with Latin America, including the support of state-regulated capitalism initiatives in line with the spirit and philosophy of the New Deal and more generally, with its Good Neighbor Policy (Helleiner 2009). The Good Neighbor policy included 'a more active idea of an inter-American financial partnership to promote economic development across Latin America' (Helleiner 2014: 29). This cooperation agenda was primarily driven by the economic and strategic interests of the US and particularly by the fear of the growing German influence in Latin America. Also, Latin American countries had, since the Great Depression, pushed for international

---

[4] The term 'money doctor' refers to experts on monetary matters providing advice to foreign governments on central bank and financial system reform. The French economist Jean Gustave Courcelle-Seneuil (1813–92) is regarded as the first monetary doctor (Flandreau 2003). These experts were in many ways the precursors of the International Monetary Fund (IMF) missions that followed the Bretton Woods agreement.

[5] In fact, Prebisch's influence on Triffin was great, including on Triffin's views on the Bretton Woods agreements. Endres (2005: 108) argues that: '[p]rior to reflecting on BW [Bretton Woods] arrangements Triffin had spent most of the period 1943–46 studying Latin American monetary problems. During that time he had been strongly influenced by the work of Raúl Prebisch [sic]. Later Triffin viewed his own reaction to BW, perhaps in part because of Prebisch's (sic) influence, as providing 'some highly unorthodox policy advice account transactions for the newly born International Monetary Fund'. In that respect it is worth noticing that White also had been a Money Doctor in Latin America, but as Helleiner (2014: 26) notes: 'Triffin ... did much more than White to reach out for advice and assistance to Latin American experts, most notably Prebisch. Triffin was also more successful than White had been in Cuba: his advice was immediately adopted by the Paraguayan government which saw its monetary reforms as key for its developmental ambitions.'

cooperation and multilateral solutions to global finance issues and for the creation of institutions for international development.

The Great Depression not only had devastating social and economic effects in Latin America, but also revealed the existing interlinkages in finance and trade across nations. Examples of Latin American initiatives for the creation of international institutions include the proposal for the creation of a multilateral banking institution for the Americas in 1931 based on the Bank for International Settlements (BIS), the advocacy for international economic cooperation at the World Economic Conference in London in 1933, and later at the Seventh Inter-American Conference in Montevideo. Establishing an Inter-American Economic Bank became a standing demand of Latin American countries throughout the 1930s and early 1940s, and provided the inspiration for Harry Dexter White's International Stabilization Fund (Steil 2013: 377–8). White provided a copy of the first draft of the Stabilization Fund to Mexican officials in 1942 for comments prior to its official circulation the following year. US government officials highly valued Mexico's opinion on White's plan as attested by the continuous interaction and discussion between both governments.

The British viewed the construction of the post-WWII order as an Anglo-American initiative and were less inclined to support the participation of developing countries, including those of Latin America and the Caribbean, in the design of the international financial architecture. Keynes's first reaction to the US' invitation of forty-four countries, which included nineteen Latin American and Caribbean nations, for the Bretton Woods conference was that the bulk of these 'have no power of commitment or final decision and everything is to be *ad referendum*' and that at least half of the countries invited including those of Latin America and the Caribbean had either nothing to contribute or knew little or nothing of international finance. In fact, as Keynes put it, Bretton Woods amounted to: '[t]he staging of a vast monkey-house ... in order that the President can say that 44 nations have agreed on the Fund and the Bank' (Keynes 1980b: 63). Nonetheless, the British embassy in Washington ensured that a copy of Keynes's plan was sent to all representatives of Latin America who attended that meeting. The British Government also made an important effort to spread the Keynes plan involving visits to several Latin American countries to explain the plan.

The most important Latin American absentee at the Bretton Woods conference was Argentina. Argentina was excluded by the US, with the tacit agreement of Britain, from the planning of the post-war world, as a result its policy of neutrality towards the Axis countries.[6] Also, Argentina was excluded from the consultation process leading to the Bretton Woods conference. One glaring example is the fact that Argentina was not included in the calculations of quotas implied by Keynes's and White's plans for the initial members of the Bretton Woods institutions prepared by the British delegation in May 1944.

As part of this process of isolation, the Argentine government did not receive copies of the Keynes and White plans. This was a cause of deep concern among Argentine officials. In fact, in April 1943, both the Minister of Finance of Argentina and Prebisch, before he was forced out of the BCRA, requested information from the US ambassador to Argentina on the stabilization plans of Keynes and White. In turn, the US ambassador referred the matter to the US Secretary of Foreign Affairs who replied: '[o]n March 4, 1943, Secretary Morgenthau addressed the following letter to the Ministers of Finance of the United Nations and to countries associated with them, including all the American Republics except (repeat except) Argentina.'[7] The available evidence points to the fact that Pinedo and Prebisch probably obtained the requested information on the Keynes and White plans from British channels.

4.3 Keynes's and White's Plans in the Periphery

Prebisch's analysis of Keynes's and White's plans indicates that overall, he thought that they were compatible with his views on monetary policy autonomy in the periphery.[8] He argued that these shared maintaining the level of

---

[6] Escudé (2006: 2–4) argues that: 'Argentine neutrality was not intrinsically pro-Axis (as official USA rhetoric held), but basically pro-British (and anti-American) instead' and that 'action against Argentina was considerably more severe than analogous action towards other neutrals, despite the fact that Argentina was contributing more to the war effort than weak belligerents, through food supplies'. It is worth noticing that this anti-Argentinean view, preceded the 1943 military *coup*, that would bring Juan Domingo Perón to the Ministry of Labor and the vice presidency, which was decidedly against American imperialism. Dosman (2008: 232) notes how after being offered a position at the IMF, Prebisch, who had been fired by the military government, was opposed by the US Treasury, and the offer was withdrawn, even though Prebisch was clearly out of favour with the Argentine government that rose up with the *coup*.

[7] Cited in Kedar (2010).

[8] It is worth noticing that Prebisch was well acquainted with Keynes's ideas on effective demand at least since 1933, and would a few years later, in 1947, publish a short guide to Keynes's ideas. In that sense, his economic views were to a great degree in accordance with Keynes and White, even if some specific differences of interpretation existed between his framework and that of Keynes, and even other Keynesians. See Pérez Caldentey and Vernengo (2016).

economic activity as a key priority which implied controlling for the growth of imports. As long as the plans provided some type of financial mechanism to pay for these imports, there was no incompatibility between the plans and a national monetary autonomy policy. He also explained that since credit was not provided in unlimited quantities, having the levers to compress imports, with the utilization of exchange controls when necessary, would allow for the adequate functioning of the plans. Since controls would affect only certain categories of imports, these would have no impact on the national or international price levels.

Prebisch thought that the organization of an international monetary system based on the granting of credit was not new. The novelty of both Keynes's ICU proposal and White's Stabilization Fund resided in the organization of an anti-cyclical international system (Prebisch 1944a [1991]: 189–91, 1944: 237–8, 242–3). In this sense, both plans were a big improvement over the gold standard system which granted credit but on a pro-cyclical basis expanding liquidity in the upward phase of the cycle and contracting it during the downward phase of the economic cycle. Prebisch and Keynes shared an aversion to the gold standard. Prebisch became very critical of the gold standard following the onset of the Great Depression and its devastating effects in Latin America.[9]

As a logical corollary, Prebisch favoured Keynes's idea of altering the value of gold, which he termed an idea of great logical force, over White's 'absolute orthodox idea of maintaining the indestructible value of gold and that of foreign currencies' (Prebisch 1944: 243). He recognized however, that altering the value of gold would require 'great international prestige on the part of the international monetary authorities that administer the Fund, in order to avoid adverse psychological consequences as those that occur each time that gold is mingled with, which is highly ingrained in the international monetary affairs' (Prebisch 1944: 242). Overall, Prebisch preferred the

---

[9] Prebisch was already critical of the automatic view of the functioning of the gold standard and the notion that the economic cycle in Argentina was essentially connected to the fluctuations of monetary aggregates in the early 1920s. In fact, he cut his teeth in the political debate by arguing that Argentina should not return to the gold standard at the pre-war parity, disagreeing with the leader and founder of the Socialist Party, Juan B. Justo (Dosman 2008: 35). Subsequently he read and translated a book written by Harvard Professor John H. Williams, that suggested that the balance of payments, and the external accounts were the key to the economic cycles in Argentina, ideas that would significantly influence Prebisch (Ibid: 35). He also met Williams in Buenos Aires in 1934, and became friends. On Williams influence on Prebisch see Brenta (2017).

ICU proposal to the Stabilization Fund, which obviously pleased Keynes.[10] Prebisch thought that the Clearing Union proposal reflected 'the elegance, audacity, and imaginative force that characterizes the economic thought of Keynes' (Prebisch 1944: 237). He argued that the idea underlying the Currency Union proposal, that is the generalization of the banking principle, the necessary equality of credits and debits (Keynes 1980a: 44–5), or closed monetary circuit, in Prebisch's words, was a bright idea (Prebisch 1944a [1991]: 205). He also was of the view that a limited liability fund such as White's Stabilization Fund would encourage a race among countries to obtain financial resources leading them to pursue unnecessary expansionary policies.

At the same time that Prebisch praised certain logical and general aspects of the international monetary plans, he thought that they did not include a mechanism that could ensure the attainment of international equilibrium in the balance of payments. Fulfilling this condition required abiding by one principle, namely, that any increase in the monetary circulation within an economy resulting from an increase in exports must spill over into an increased demand for imports. Given their importance in the world economy and global trade, the adequate functioning of a closed system of credits and debits required the compliance of developed countries, and, particularly, of the US with the rules of the game.

According to Prebisch, in the period following WWII, the US took on the role of the cyclical centre of the world. The cyclical centre referred to the country, or perhaps group of countries, whose economic repercussions due to its importance were transmitted to the rest of the world. In the nineteenth century and up until WWI, Great Britain was the cyclical centre only to be overtaken by the US thereafter, as Britain became indebted in dollars.[11] The countries subject to the influence of the impulses of the centre, the periphery, included all Latin American countries. As Prebisch put it (Prebisch 1946 [1993]: 224):

> The United States ... fulfills the role of the main cyclical centre, not only within the continent but also in the world: and the Latin American countries are in the periphery of the economic system ... Why do I call the United States, the cyclical centre? Because from this country, given its

[10] Keynes learned of Prebisch's preference for his plan from British officials and 'declared that the news was exceptionally important'. See Helleiner (2014: 158).

[11] Prebisch's views here can be seen as similar and preceding the notion of hegemonic stability currency discussed by Kindleberger (1973).

magnitude and economic characteristics, start the expansionary and contractionary impulses of world economic life and particularly those of the Latin American periphery, whose countries are under the influence of those impulses just as they had been before, when Great Britain had the role of main cyclical center.

Within this context the only way in which countries on the periphery which, due to their economic structure happened also to be deficit countries, could increase their exports in a sufficient degree to boost their economic growth and pay for their credits was through an expansionary policy in the cyclical centre, the US. In its absence, the countries in the periphery could only deal with external imbalance by compressing imports through a contraction in economic activity. Hence, Prebisch (1944: 245) argued: '[t]his is why I insist on the fundamental point that I have so many times mentioned: I consider of capital importance for reconstruction of the economy and of the world monetary system, more than plans of this nature, full employment plans in the main advanced countries in the world and especially in the United States.' Prebisch thought that the US economy was distant from a full employment situation and that it faced significant obstacles to its achievement.

First there was a question of sovereignty. Full employment was a requirement for the adequate functioning of the international monetary plans rather than an internal policy decision. Thus prioritizing this policy objective meant subjecting internal policy decisions to the dictates of the international economy. Second, and more importantly, a policy of full employment, within the system of generous granting of credit envisaged in Keynes's Clearing Union coupled with what Prebisch termed its 'automatism', prompted fears of inflation which discouraged following expansionary policy objectives. Automatism referred to 'the facility to use international credit without deliberation or direction conducive to equilibrium' (Prebisch 1944a [1991]: 195). Automatism was a characteristic of Keynes's plan, as the credit would not be used according to the situation in the world economy, but rather according to the quotas provided to each country. As Prebisch argued: 'within wide limits there would be a complete indetermination regarding the intensity with which new purchasing power is created, with serious consequences, first on the economy of the United States ... and then on the rest of the world due to its natural repercussion' (1944a [1991]: 195). Thus, one of the main positive aspects of Keynes's plan, that is, the facility to use international credit also entailed for Prebisch its gravest danger.

In this sense, Prebisch thought that Keynes's plan shared the same weakness as the gold standard, which was also a system based on automatism, and this could lead, as in the case of the gold standard, to its own destruction.[12] Other economists at the time, in Brazil, Chile, and Mexico, including Eugênio Gudin, Otávio Gouveia de Bulhões, Herman Max Coers, Eduardo Villaseñor Ángeles, also saw in Keynes's plan an inflation-prone scheme that did not further impose the required discipline on debtors.[13] Prebisch concluded:

> I do not believe in any automatic system of credit, neither domestic or international, because I believe in a centralized system ... I am convinced that nothing can be constructed in international monetary affairs within the play of an automatic system. A high degree of highly efficient management on the part of the authorities responsible for the provision of international credit, according to countries' needs and those of the world economy, is the reason why I conceive inconvenient any automatic system.
>
> (Prebisch 1944: 241)

A second important critique voiced by Prebisch concerned the limits placed by the international monetary plan on policy autonomy and, in particular, on the capacity of the periphery to pursue expansionary policies, which he illustrated with the case of Argentina. Prebisch complained that the monetary plans viewed the economic and monetary phenomena of all countries through the same prism, failing to distinguish the inequality of situations between centre and periphery. Not all countries could adopt the same monetary policy and directives. One important difference between centre and periphery was their sensitivity to imports. The countries in the periphery needed to import capital equipment, machinery, and even key raw materials, and inputs, to build up their infrastructure, boost their productivity and output growth potential. In other words, their income elasticity of imports was very high, and as a result, any expansionary policy would leak

---

[12] These views were similar to Williams's ideas, and perhaps Prebisch was somewhat influenced by his views. It is worth noticing in this respect that Williams was somewhat sceptical about Keynesian ideas (Endres 2005: 56).

[13] Note that Keynes did not see inflation in the post-war period as being demand driven, but rather as a supply bottleneck phenomenon. Before drawing up his Keynes plan, he mentioned price controls for inflation control in January 1942, suggesting that: 'The avoidance of inflationary conditions in the immediate post-war period should be provided ... not by of credit deflation or currency pressures, but by the continuance of ... controls on raw materials and other products' (Keynes 1980a: 105). His commodity control scheme which was already incorporated into its post-war plan also served to control prices.

into an increased demand for imports, even below a full employment position. The case of the centre was markedly different; below full employment an expansionary policy would first spill into the domestic economy and only slowly affect the growth of imports.

At the same time, countries in the periphery faced lower export elasticities of income than advanced economies, and especially relative to the US. For Prebisch, the available empirical evidence revealed that any increase in the purchase of goods and services in the US from the rest of the world tended to increase the purchase of goods and services of the rest of the world from the US. Contrarily, in the periphery, as in the case of Argentina, increasing imports would not generate a rise in exports. He explained this on the basis of the small share of Argentina in world trade. According to Prebisch, Argentinean imports represented 17.1 per cent of the total income of the country, whereas the imports of the rest of world from Argentina accounted for only 0.3 per cent of its global income. The combination of high-income elasticity of imports and low export elasticity of income, relative to advanced economies and the US, set the conditions for a chronic tendency to balance of payments disequilibrium.

This imbalance could temporarily be confronted through the type of credit envisaged in Keynes's Clearing Union proposal, but would ultimately put pressure on the stock of international reserves. And this was another difference between the centre and the periphery – advanced economies, and particularly the US, possessed ample stocks of gold. In fact, as much as the pound was the de facto key currency before WWI, the dollar had become for all practical purposes the key currency, if not after the war, at least with the Tripartite Agreement in 1936, which stabilized the exchange rates of the US, the UK, and France. This was not the case in Argentina. Hence, any increase in aggregate demand and imports, could, in the absence of a concomitant rise in exports, threaten its international reserve position. This led peripheral economies to forego growth and employment gains in order to maintain financial stability. The increased demand for reserve currencies for precautionary purposes is evidence that financial stability remains to this day a fundamental policy goal of governments in developing countries.

As a result, the periphery does not have at its disposal the same monetary toolkit as the centre with which to face business cycles. These arguments led Prebisch to push for his proposal for exchange controls for imports as a way to isolate the Argentine economy from the ups and downs of the external sector. As he put it (Prebisch 1946 (1993): 225–6):

[T]here is a marked difference between monetary phenomena in the cyclical center and the periphery ... The situation of the cyclical center, if it is suffering from a strong decline in prices, has in its own hands the expansionary resources to ensure their recovery, without concern for its monetary parities; the cyclical center does not need to move the parity of its currency to act on prices. On the contrary the countries of the periphery cannot by themselves initiate an expansionary movement, because immediately these would have to end it due to the impressive decline in their international reserves .... unless these can have recourse to other means such as exchange controls or the movement in exchange parities to avoid drastic consequences.

Thus, given the hierarchy of economic power and currencies, and marked differences in economic structures, the countries of the periphery had no choice but to turn to instruments such as exchange controls, to pursue expansionary policies and insulate their economies from the fluctuations of the global economy. Yet, it was precisely this policy option that the monetary framework of the international plans severely limited and curtailed. According to both Keynes's ICU and White's Stabilization Fund a country could not alter its exchange rate without the consent of the international monetary authorities.

Hence as Prebisch put it: 'will we dispose ... of our monetary sovereignty, of our faculty to move the exchange rates in accordance with our appreciation of internal and external conditions of the country, for a plate of lentils? Or will we delegate that privative faculty in an international mechanism? I think that ... public opinion will not accept such a decision' (Prebisch 1944a [1991]: 201). It is important to note that Prebisch did not favour exchange controls for exports because their impact would be minimal relative to the fluctuations in international markets. In view of the limitations of the Keynes and White plans, Prebisch argued that a feasible alternative could be provided by Williams's 'Key Currency' alternative (Williams 1944).[14] Williams's plan was less ambitious in terms of the provision of credit

---

[14] Prebisch had a long-standing friendship with Williams dating back to the 1920s, as noted above (Dosman 2001: 89–105; Brenta 2017). Williams and Dexter White studied under Frank Taussig at Harvard and both tested some of the main hypotheses of the neoclassical adjustment mechanism in their dissertations (Bordo and Schwartz 1984). Williams's work focused on Argentina in the period 1880–1900 and highlighted important limitations in the traditional adjustment mechanism based on relative prices (Williams 1920).

than Keynes's ICU and lacked its inherent automatism. At the same time, it avoided the rigidity that characterized White's plan.[15]

4.4 Prebisch and the Other Outsiders

While Williams was invited to Bretton Woods as an observer, his partici-pation would have been conditioned by his defence of the American Plan, something he decided he could not do. In his own words, during the Senate Committee on Banking and Currency hearing on the international mone-tary system, in 1945: 'I had fault to find with the experts' report and wanted to continue to be free to think about the problem' (Williams, in Endres 2005: 62). Williams provided a similar critique to that provided by Prebisch of the Bretton Woods plans, which were based on the principle of the equality of currencies. The monetary plans viewed the post-war world order as sym-metrical consisting in a set of national currencies operating on a plane of equality within a central coordination mechanism, whether it be the ICU, the Stabilization Fund, or the eventually created International Monetary Fund IMF), whose formal function would be to provide liquidity to supple-ment international reserves. The principle of the equality of currencies 'had its counterpart in the notion of the equality of countries' (Endres 2005: 63). Economic size and economic structure were not relevant to the international monetary plans (Williams 1943).

For Williams, as for Prebisch, economic and monetary phenomena were different in countries with the key currencies, such as the US and the UK, than in those countries with less relevant currencies that were not used as vehicle currencies in international trade and finance and the same rules could not apply to both. Within this logic, there could not be a single mon-etary organization that could respond to the needs of countries that were structurally heterogeneous. As he explained (Williams 1944: xvii):

> One of my basic notions about international trade and monetary theory for many years has been that we must take into account that this is a hetero-geneous world made up of countries unlike in kind, of different economic

---

[15] The issue of the autonomy of domestic economic policy was central to Latin American delegations in the discussions of both plans and at the Bretton Woods conference. The delega-tions of the region emphasized the need to create mechanisms to stabilize commodity prices, to have greater exchange rate flexibility, to have the possibility of imposing capital controls, and to be able to protect nascent industries (Helleiner 2014: 169–72).

weight in the general scheme of trade and financial organization, and in different stages of economic development. I have long doubted whether any single type of monetary organization or of monetary and trade policy is applicable to all. This has been my objection to what I have called the textbook type of gold standard and [has been] the root idea of what I have called the key currencies approach to international economic organization.

Williams sustained that maintaining international monetary and trade stability in a heterogeneous world, organized along multilateral lines, required that countries adopt different responsibilities according to their size, development, and importance within the global economy. He argued that monetary and trade stability called for a compromise with a hard core two-sided external and internal adjustment falling mainly on the bigger and more advanced economies, whose performance 'dominated and determined what happened to all other countries' (Williams 1943, 1944: 16). The larger and more developed economies should have the responsibility of cooperating among themselves to maintain a high level of real income and high level of exchange rate stability. For Williams: '[i]f this could be done, the problem of maintaining exchange stability for the other countries, and a reasonable state of economic well-being within them, would probably not present major difficulties' (1944: 19).

Cooperation implied, for key currency countries, avoiding any type of trade or exchange rate restrictions. The performance of a country like the US depended on the state of its domestic economy and not on its foreign trade. In the case of the UK, Williams recognized the importance of its external sector for the rest of the economy but argued that the country had as much of an obligation as the US to 'maintain monetary stability and to practice the rules of multilateral trading' (Williams 1944: xix).[16]

The case of developing economies was an entirely different story. Williams's characterization of developing countries is very similar to that provided by Prebisch. Young countries, as he referred to them, and, more specifically young agricultural countries, were highly dependent on foreign trade and much more so than any developed country. Moreover, due to their narrow production structure, absence of diversification, and the small size of

---

[16] Williams proposed initially to stabilize the exchange rate between the dollar and the pound and dictate measures to cooperate in domestic policy matters. Prebisch thought that the problems concerning the relationship between the dollar and the pound in relation to European currencies which were difficult and diverse should be addressed at a later date. See (Prebisch 1944: 262.)

their domestic market, the income flows generated by exports would tend to overspill towards increased imports. There was in Williams's analysis a tacit assumption, which was more explicit in Prebisch's writings, that the periphery combined a high import elasticity of demand with low export elasticity relative to the larger and more advanced economies. The resulting chronic tendency to balance of payments disequilibrium in the developing economies would place an important constraint on their possibilities to expand demand and reach their full employment potential.

The performance of developing countries depended 'on the maintenance of good markets for their products in the advanced countries, which means upon high production and employment in those countries' (Williams 1944: xix). This would provide the space for the former to confront the short-term fluctuations in the business cycle as well as to focus on their long-term development. According to Williams, the structural features of developing countries and their subordinate position in the global economy provided the rationale to argue that these economies should not be subject to the same market discipline as developed countries. He thought, at first, that developing countries should have the leeway to vary their exchange rates according to their balance-of-payments requirements. Their economies would benefit the most from varying their exchange rates, given the importance of trade for their economic performance, while at the same time due to their small importance in the world economy variations in the rates would have the least negative consequences for other countries. This, of course, suggests that Williams had a great degree of confidence in the ability of exchange rates to resolve balance of payments disequilibria, and his general confidence in neoclassical, or marginalist, adjustment mechanisms (Endres 2005: 56).

In the end, Williams opted for exchange controls in line with Prebisch, out of a pragmatic view that assumed that there was significant difference between the model and reality.[17] Exchange controls, and more to the point, the use of import licences was a more effective method than varying the exchange rate, and the use of tariffs. It was simply more effective, precise, and flexible, with the least negative impact on other economies (Williams 1934, 1936, 1944: xx, 196–7, 222–3). Williams concluded (1944: xx):

---

[17] Endres (2005: 57) notes how Williams was one of the first to argue that while the automatic gold standard model worked well in theory, in reality the classic gold standard was a sterling or pound-based system that required management from the centre. Of course, this view echoes Keynes's notion that the Bank of England was like the conductor of an orchestra during the gold standard, fundamentally managing the system with changes of the rate of interest.

Such practices [exchange controls] are, of course, a departure from the strict principles of multilateral free trading, but as I have sought to indicate the problem by its essential nature is one of compromise, and I can see no reason a priori for barring this one out [exchange controls] and letting others [protective tariffs] in. It becomes a question of the predominance of forces, policies, and practices at work in the world, as a whole, and these depend fundamentally upon the policies of the key countries.

Williams shared with Keynes the view that currency and exchange stabilization was only one aspect of post-WWII economic and financial reform. In addition to the ICU, Keynes proposed an international investment institution to provide funds for reconstruction and development purposes, a commodity buffer stock mechanism, and an international commercial policy that allowed for the expansion of trade (Keynes 1980a: 60). Williams agreed with Keynes that international monetary stability and thus a monetary proposal should have priority and precedence over the rest of the institutions that would form the international economic architecture after WWII (Williams 1943, 1944: 21; Keynes 1980b: 5).

The views of Prebisch and Williams were echoed in the writings of another outsider in the discussion on the international monetary system, namely, Michał Kalecki. His views on the international monetary plans of Keynes and White and on the problem of international monetary stabilization and coordination also raise some of the limitations of the official plans (Kalecki and Schumacher 1943; Kalecki 1946).[18] Kalecki and Schumacher (1943: 29) criticized the concept of international equilibrium underlying Keynes's and White's plans. Both these plans assumed that international monetary stability depended on achieving current account equilibrium for all countries. However, this ignored the fact that countries forming part of a multilateral arrangement did not have the same levels of development and, thus, obviously, even though Kalecki does not mention it specifically, the same size, structural features, and importance in the world economy.

Different levels of development entailed that the world trading system was composed of surplus and deficit countries. Current equilibrium could be achieved by pressuring surplus countries to export less and/or import more or by pushing countries to increase their exports and/or curtail their

[18] For an exposition of the view of Kalecki on the monetary order after WWII and on Keynes's and White's plans see Toporowski (2018a) and (2018b), and Chapter 3.

imports. In practice, international equilibrium would be achieved through contractionary policies, as deficit countries contract their imports, and surplus countries, by definition, would have lower exports. Kalecki and Schumacher's analysis points to a fundamental contradiction in the logic of the monetary plans including that of Keynes. Keynes conceived the ICU as a plan to put an 'expansionist, in place of a contractionist pressure of world trade' (Keynes 1980a: 46). But, contrary to design, the objective of achieving international current account equilibrium applied within a heterogeneous world would lead to the exact opposite result.

Kalecki and Schumacher proposed replacing the current account equilibrium with what they called unbalanced equilibrium; that is the current account plus long-term capital flows or the basic balance of the balance of payments, in fact, integrating the real and monetary sides of the balance of payments. A multilateral arrangement could realize its potential if all countries were allowed to pursue full employment policies, on the basis of aggregate domestic demand expansion and on foreign net expenditure financed by long-term loans. In other words, 'each country must maintain such a domestic expenditure that this expenditure plus export surplus financed by foreign lending (or minus export deficit financed by foreign borrowing) is adequate to assure full employment' (Kalecki 1946: 325). An international investment board, which was a part of Keynes's ICU plan, would decide the amount of long-term loans provided to deficit countries. In this way Kalecki and Schumacher's plan combined clearing, as with Keynes's scheme, with lending to solve simultaneously the problems related to world trade and investment.

The plan addressed the situation of three types of countries. The first comprised the surplus countries. In their view, countries whose objective was to have an export surplus should not be penalized for accumulating metallic reserves, gold, or the international unit of account, bancor, in Keynes's proposal, but for all practical purposes in the immediate post-war the US dollar.[19] The second type included countries that needed external finance to compensate for their current account deficit due to reconstruction, and

---

[19] Kalecki and Schumacher (1943) also argued that discouraging countries from achieving balance of trade surpluses would restrict exports and 'slow down the advancement of developing countries' (p. 31). Also, deficit countries should be granted a symmetric treatment to that of creditor countries, and should not be penalized. By channelling imports towards countries needing an import surplus 'for purpose of reconstruction, readjustment and industrialization' and those whose external deficit is due to other reasons, the international investment board would relieve balance of trade pressures and protect them from a deterioration in their international liquidity position.

readjustment for industrialization purposes. The purpose relating to this group of countries was to safeguard their long-term liquidity. Finally, the third type of countries comprised countries whose deficit responded to reasons that excluded those arising out of reconstruction, readjustment, or industrialization. In this case, the objective would focus on maintaining a long-term balance in their current account. This could be achieved by using the power of the investment board to 'direct borrowers receiving development loans to use them fully or partly for increasing imports' from this group of countries (Kalecki and Schumacher 1943: 32). The flows directed through the investment board would be complementary to other types of long-term lending, and the greater their volume, the greater would be the possibility of closing the existing imbalances in the private sector.

While Kalecki was not in favour of exchange rate intervention for what he called full employment countries, he argued that licensing of imports to prevent the rise in prices of those commodities affected by supply restrictions was fully compatible with multilateralism, as long as the controls aimed to change the composition of imports and were not used as a discriminatory tool (Kalecki 1946: 324). More importantly, perhaps, it is worth remembering that while Prebisch and Williams were somewhat concerned with the possibility of inflationary pressures, caused by the automatism of the Bretton Woods agreement, Kalecki (1943) had already understood that the post-war world would be one of stop and go, associated with what he called the political aspects of full employment policies. He understood that full employment policies would create a backlash among capitalists, since full employment would empower the working class, and that would bring cyclically calls for austerity.[20]

Further, it is worth mentioning that Keynes's plan was, in fact, defeated at Bretton Woods, and that White's Stabilization Fund with the dollar as the key currency, rather than the Clearing Union and bancor, was the one implemented, with Keynes presiding over the less relevant debates about the World Bank, while White led the discussions about the creation of the IMF.

---

[20] In this respect it is worth noticing, as Toporowski (2013: 35) does that: '[a]fter the death of Keynes in 1946, Joan Robinson taught three generations of Cambridge University economists that not only had Keynes been anticipated by Kalecki's 1933 business cycle analysis and studies of wages and employment, but also that the latter was the "more consistent" Keynesian.' In other words, Kalecki, more than Keynes, but also more than Prebisch or Williams, was concerned with the need to maintain public investment as a tool for full employment, and he thought that in developing countries planning would play that role.

If social cohesion was necessary, in Kalecki's view, to promote full employment in advanced economies, the working of the international monetary system required a Marshall Plan and significant injections of US dollars, something that was suggested by Williams (Endres 2005: 68).

The limitations of the Bretton Woods system were evident to the three outsiders. Kalecki and Kowalik (1971: 472) would go on to note, as the system drew to its end, that expansion of the welfare state and full employment in the centre would turn the working class, as they suggested, 'radically reformist in its attitude towards capitalism', rather than revolutionary. This opened the space for more militant pro-capitalist views even within the lower classes, something that would eventually occur with the rise of neoliberalism and the collapse of the so-called Golden Age of Capitalism (King 2013). As the first Secretary General of the United Nations Conference on Trade and Development (UNCTAD), Prebisch would also eventually become frustrated with American plans for development in the region. After the Cuban Revolution those plans became more focused on the Alliance for Progress and the creation of the Inter-American Development Bank (IADB), and would move to a more global rather than Latin American approach to economic development. Even though Bretton Woods was eventually successful in restoring multilateralism and seen as a glorious period of economic growth and prosperity, it would not be out of place to suggest that it was so in spite rather than as a result of the arrangements that were formalized in New Hampshire, and that the outsiders were for the most part correct in their critiques.

4.5 Conclusion

For a good part of his life, Keynes thought of himself as an outsider, at least from the time he left the peace negotiations in Versailles until WWII, a period in which he warned like a Cassandra about the mistakes made by policymakers, like the return to the gold standard, the doomed belief in the automatism of markets, and their reliance on the self-adjusting mechanism to solve the Great Depression without public works. But during the two wars he was effectively at the centre of economic policymaking at the global level. His plan for the international monetary system after WWII might have been defeated. But he had a seat at the table, and he went on to defend it in his speech to the House of Lords (Keynes 1980b: 4–6, 9–23). Prebisch, on the other hand, had been at the centre of economic policymaking in Argentina during the Great Depression, and his somewhat heterodox actions at the head of the BCRA, including some counter-cyclical policies and the use of exchange controls to minimize external problems helped Argentina recover relatively fast, and without defaulting on foreign obligations.

However, when the plans for the international monetary system were being drafted, he developed, as an outsider, his own ideas on how the international monetary system should work, not only because he was expelled from policy circles in Argentina, but also because the country was excluded from debates on the new international financial architecture. Between 1943 and 1949, after leaving the BCRA and before moving to ECLAC, he was to some extent like Keynes trying to influence the debate from the sidelines. Prebisch's views on the limitations of Keynes's and White's plans owe a great deal to Williams's critiques of the plans, and bear some resemblance to the views developed by Kalecki. Prebisch, Williams, and Kalecki all believed that a symmetric understanding of the adjustment process that did not take into consideration the significant differences between what Prebisch called the centre and the periphery were doomed to fail. In particular, balance of payments problems in the periphery would make catching-up impossible. They were ultimately correct in prophesying the limits of Bretton Woods, like Keynes, who wanted to title his book *Essays in Persuasion and Prophecy*, since his prophesying proved to be more successful than his ability to persuade.

Acknowledgements

The authors are Coordinators of the Unit of Financing for Development, Economic Development Division (ECLAC), Santiago, Chile (esteban.perez@cepal.org) and Professor of Economics (Bucknell University) (mv012@bucknell.edu). The opinions here expressed are the authors' own and may not coincide with the institutions with which they are affiliated. A draft of this paper was presented at the seminar 'Michal Kalecki and the Problem of International Equilibrium' (OECD, 26 September 2019). The authors would like to thank the valuable comments provided by Jerzy Osiatyński and Jan Toporowski. The compiled works of Prebisch before 1949 comprise four volumes and are referred to in the text as Raúl Prebisch, Obras (RPO) jointly with the respective volumes (I–IV). All the quotations of Prebisch's works in English are translations by the authors of this paper.

References

Bordo, Michael D., and Schwartz, Anna J. 1984 *A retrospective on the classical gold standard, 1821–1931*. Chicago: University of Chicago Press.

Brenta, Noemí 2017 'Las coincidencias del pensamiento de John H. Williams y Raúl Prebisch acerca del orden económico internacional de posguerra'. (Similarities in John Williams's and Raúl Prebisch's Thought about the International Monetary Order after the War). *América Latina en la Historia Económica* (Mayo-Agosto): Vol 24, no. 2, 235–38.

Dosman, Edgar J. 2001 'Markets and the State in the evolution of the "Prebisch manifesto"' *Cepal Review* No. 75, pp. 87–102.

Dosman, Edgar J. 2008 *The Life and Times of Raúl Prebisch 1901–1986*. Montreal: McGill-Queen's University Press.

Endres, Anthony M. 2005 *Great Architects of International Finance. The Bretton Woods Era*. New York: Routledge.

Escudé, Carlos 2006 'The US Destabilization and Economic Boycott of Argentina of the 1940s, revisited'. Universidad del CEMA, Serie de Documentos de Trabajo No 323.

Flandreau, M. 2003 'Introduction: Money and doctors', in M Flandreau (ed.) *Money Doctors: The Experience of International Financial Advising 1850–2000*. New York: Routledge, pp. 1–9.

Harberler, Gottfried 1947 'Comments on "National Central Banking and the International Economy"', in L. Metzler, R. Triffin and G. Haberler (eds.) *International Monetary Policies*. Washington, DC: Board of Governors of the United States Federal Reserve, pp. 82–102.

Helleiner, Eric 2009 'Central Bankers as Good Neighbours: US Money Doctors in Latin America during the 1940s', *Financial History Review* 16(1): 5–25.

Helleiner, Eric 2014 *Forgotten Foundations of Bretton Woods*. Ithaca, NY: Cornell University Press.

Kalecki, Michał 1943 'Political Aspects of Full Employment', in M. Kalecki (ed.). *The Last Phase in the Transformation of Capitalism*. New Delhi: Aakar Books, 2011, pp. 75–83.

Kalecki, Michał 1946, 'Multilateralism and Full Employment' *Canadian Journal of Economics and Political Science*, 12(3). pp. 322–7.

Kalecki, Michał and Tadeusz Kowalik 1971 'Observations on the "Crucial Reform"', in Jerzy Osiatyński (ed.) *Collected Works of Michał Kalecki, Volume II, Capitalism: Business Cycles and Full Employment*. Oxford: Clarendon Press, 1990, pp. 467–476.

Kalecki, Michał and Ernst F. Schumacher 1943 'International Clearing and Long-Term Lending', *Bulletin of the Institute of Statistics Oxford Supplement* 5(5): 29–33.

Kedar, Claudia 2010 'The Beginning of a Controversial Relationship: The IMF, the World Bank, and Argentina, 1943–46', *Canadian Journal of Latin American and Caribbean Studies* 35(69): 201–30.

Keynes, John Maynard 1980a *The Collected Writings of John Maynard Keynes. Vol. XXV. Activities 1940–1944. Shaping the Post-War World: The Clearing Union*, edited by Donald E. Moggridge. New York: Cambridge University Press.

Keynes, John Maynard 1980b *The Collected Writings of John Maynard Keynes. Vol. XXVI. Activities 1941–1946. Shaping the Post-War World: Bretton Woods and Reparations*, edited by Donald E. Moggridge. New York: Cambridge University Press.

Kindleberger, Charles P. 1973 *The World in Depression, 1929–1939*. Oakland, CA: University of California Press.

King, John E. 2013 'Whatever Happened to the "Crucial Reform"?', in Riccardo Bellofiore, Ewa Karwowski, and Jan Toporowski (eds.) *Economic Crisis and Political Economy: Volume 2 of Essays in Honour of Tadeusz Kowalik*. Basingstoke: Palgrave Macmillan, pp. 29–41.

Llach, Juan J. 1984 'El Plan Pinedo de 1940: su significado histórico y los orígenes de la economía política del peronismo' (The Pinedo Plan of 1940: its historical significance and the origins of the political economy of Peronism) *Desarrollo Económico* 23(92): 513–55.

Nurske, Ragnar 1944 *International Currency Experience. Lessons of the Inter-War Period*. Geneva: League of Nations.

Pérez Caldentey, Esteban and Matías Vernengo 2016 'Reading Keynes in Buenos Aires: Prebisch and the Dynamics of Capitalism', *Cambridge Journal of Economics* 40(6): 1725–41.

Pérez Caldentey, Esteban and Matías Vernengo 2019 'Raúl Prebisch y su faceta de banquero central y doctor monetario: Textos publicados e inéditos en la década de 1940', *ECLAC Review* (Suplemento Especial 129):Vol. 26 pp. 9–41.

Prebisch, Raúl 1943 *La moneda y el ritmo de actividad económica*. [Money and Economic Activity] Unpublished.

Prebisch, Raúl 1944 *El Patrón Oro y los Ciclos Monetarios en la Argentina* [The Gold Standard and Monetary Cycles in Argentina] Vols-I-II. Unpublished.

Prebisch, Raúl 1944a [1991] 'La Política Monetaria Nacional y Los Planes Monetarios Internacionales', [National Monetary Policy and the International Monetary Plans] in Raúl Prebisch *Obras 1919–1949 Vol. III*. Buenos Aires: Fundación Raúl Prebisch, pp. 189–206.

Prebisch, Raúl 1944b [1991] 'La Política Monetaria Interna' [Domestic Monetary Policy], in Raúl Prebisch *Obras 1919–1949 Vol. III*, Buenos Aires: Fundación Raúl Prebisch, pp. 88–122.

Prebisch, Raúl 1944c [1991] 'Lineamientos de una Política Monetaria Nacional', [Guidelines for a National Monetary Policy] in Raúl Prebisch *Obras 1919–1949 Vol. III*. Buenos Aires: Fundación Raúl Prebisch, pp. 123–88.

Prebisch, Raúl 1945 [1993] 'La Experiencia Monetaria Argentina desde la Crisis Mundial y la Creación y Funcionamiento del Banco Central' [The Argentine Monetary Experience since the World Crisis and the Creation and Functioning of the Central Bank], in Raúl Prebisch *Obras 1919–1949 Vol. IV*. Buenos Aires: Fundación Raúl Prebisch, pp. 113–94.

Prebisch, R. 1946 [1993] 'Panorama General de los Problemas de Regulaciónn Monetaria y Crediticia en el Continente Americano: América Latina', [General Panorama of Monetary and Credit Regulation in the American Continent: Latin America] in Raúl Prebisch *Obras 1919–1949 Vol. IV*. Buenos Aires: Fundación Raúl Prebisch, pp. 224–31.

Steil, Benn 2013 *The Battle of Bretton Woods: John Maynard Keynes, Harry Dexter White, and the Making of a New World Order*. Princeton, NJ: Princeton University Press.

Toporowski, Jan 2013 'Tadeusz Kowalik: Radical Political Economist, Solidarity Advisor and Critic of Globalised Capitalism', *PSL Quarterly Review*. 66(264): 50–7.

Toporowski, Jan 2018a 'Multilateral and Regional Trade and Payments', in Noemi Levy and Jorge Bustamante (eds.) *Financialisation in Latin America Challenges of the Export-Led Growth Model* Abingdon: Routledge, pp. 13–22.

Toporowski, Jan 2018b *Michał Kalecki An Intellectual Biography, Volume II. By Intellect Alone 1939–1970*. Basingstoke: Palgrave.

Triffin, R. (1944), 'Central Banking and Monetary Management in Latin America', in S. Harris (ed.) *Economic Problems of Latin America*. New York, McGraw-Hill, pp. 93–116.

Williams, John H. 1920 *Argentine International Trade under Inconvertible Paper Money 1880–1900*. New York: Greenwood Press.

Williams, John H. 1934 'The World's Monetary Dilemma – Internal versus External Stability', in John H. Williams *Post-War Monetary Plans and Other Essays*, New York: Alfred A. Knopf 1944, pp. 191–8.

Williams, John H. 1936 'International Monetary Organization and Policy', in John H. Williams *Post-War Monetary Plans and Other Essays*. New York: Alfred A Knopf 1944, pp.199–227.

Williams, John H. 1943 'Currency Stabilization: The Keynes and White Plans', in John H. Williams *Post-War Monetary Plans and Other Essays*. New York: Alfred A Knopf 1944 pp. 3–21.

Williams, John H. 1944 'The Joint Monetary Plan' in John H. Williams *Post-War Monetary Plans and Other Essays*. New York: Alfred A knopf 1944 pp. xi–xxxii.

PART II

KALECKI, MULTILATERALISM, AND LONG-TERM DEVELOPMENT

5

The Rise and Fall of the Bretton Woods Systems and the Re-Emergence of Private Debt in Developing Economies

Noemi Levy-Orlik

5.1 Introduction

At the end of the World War II (WWII) important discussions around organization of the international financial system took place. The main objective of these deliberations was to build a new international financial system that would guarantee enough liquidity for international trade to take place, free of speculation (no currency wars), and based on multilateral agreements to avoid structural trade imbalances. In this financial organization public debt had the lead.

The Bretton Woods meetings sought to substitute for the previous international system based on the gold standard and free private capital movement. From those meetings emerged the monetary system after WWII with arrangement that relied on restricted capital mobility, anchored indirectly in gold reserves, and characterized as a system of 'thin' globalization (Rodrik, 2010). Additionally, this new system relied on fixed (but adjustable) exchange rates, in which a supranational entity, the International Monetary Fund (IMF), was to authorize governments to modify their exchange rates. Short-term private capital movements were to be limited at the international level. Hence the provision of international liquidity was related to international trade and would stem from government credits; and long-term finance provisions for economic growth and development would stem from international institutions such as the World Bank.

Noemi Levy-Orlik, *Bretton Woods Systems and Private Debt*. In: *International Equilibrium and Bretton Woods.* Edited by Jerzy Osiatyński and Jan Toporowski, Oxford University Press. © Oxford University Press (2022). DOI: 10.1093/oso/9780192856401.003.0006

In this chapter we argue that the international post-war financial organization (the Bretton Woods system) was dysfunctional for economic stability because private financial capital was supposed to be inactive and rested on one national currency (the US dollar), originating in the economy of the United States (US), whose external deficits provided world-wide liquidity. The Bretton Woods system adopted a fixed exchange rate structure that, although adjustable, failed to guarantee enough liquidity for international trade; and, more importantly, financial instruments to attain financial stability weren't provided. In addition, long-term loans were insufficient to finance the economic growth and development of economically backward regions. Thus, the multilateral system failed and beggar-thy-neighbour practices reappeared, along with an unregulated foreign exchange (Eurodollar) market, which at the beginning of the 1970s planted the seeds that destabilized the international financial system. This was the genesis of a new international financial order that internationalized and even globalized domestic economic structures, spreading financial and economic instability.

During the late 1960s an industrial crisis burst out in developed countries, led by huge trade imbalances, particularly in the hegemonic country of the US, along with the breakdown of the Bretton Woods system coupled with the demonetization of gold (1971). In the post-Bretton Woods financial system, private debt regained importance, whose value was not related to any commodity price, making the international financial system a fundamental space for the circulation of capitalist liquidity, not linked to savings. The main outcome of this new international system was the internationalization of liquidity, while savings were limited to domestic spheres (Borio and Disyatat 2015). In this new setting, economic policy objectives switched from full employment to price stability, reinstating monetary policy reaction functions (Taylor 1993). Output prices stabilized along with financial inflation, which distributed profits in favour of large corporations. In this scenario the movement of private capital flows was coupled with flexible exchange rates and volatile interest rates that, altogether, agitated capital markets.

The reappearance of private debt at the international level deepened external trade disequilibria. Capital markets were reactivated, not only in developed countries, but also in emerging (and developing) economies. Under these settings, Latin American economies generated *sui generis* conditions. Instead of unleashing economic growth, excess liquidity in international currency increased economic dependence on external markets, along with higher financial instability.

This chapter is divided into five sections. In Section 5.2 the proposals of Keynes and White are reviewed as well as the views of Schumacher and Kalecki on the organization of the international financial system, highlighting that the outcome of the Bretton Woods meetings was not viable in the context of the capitalist system. In Section 5.3 the effects of the demonetization of gold and the freedom of capital mobility at the international level are examined; followed by an analytical section (Section 5.4) which reviews the relationship of private debts and capital mobility in developing economies. Section 5.5 contains some final considerations.

5.2 Schumacher–Kalecki Proposals versus Keynes and White

Once WWII terminated, an important discussion took place on how to reorganize the international financial system and create conditions for economic growth and stability.[1] These would eventually include the defeated countries of WWII. In addition to the Marshall Plan, launched by the US, stable international liquidity was required to regain economic growth free of protectionist practices.

Keynes and White were committed to constructing an international financial system that would secure liquidity to finance international trade, and limit speculative activities,[2] through restricting private capital movement in the international sphere, combined with fixed exchange rates, and coupled with capital controls. In this scheme, governments were required to manage large capital flows (Rodrik 2010), in which financial capital would act as the 'servant' of productive sector needs (Russell 2008). The foundations of this economic model rested on government regulation and active public intervention in economic activity, including counter-cyclical fiscal policies, loose monetary policies guided by domestic demand, and industrialization in backward regions (Amsden 2004). Government was supposed to guarantee investment spending at full employment level (Keynes 1936).

Keynes proposed an International Clearing Union (ICU) using an international currency (bancor) organized under a quota system; which

---

[1] This section is based on Toporowski 2017.

[2] In his *General Theory* Keynes (1936) was critical of capital market operations because they set off speculative activity, especially under the domination of financial capital. The theory's main proposals were to socialize investment spending and policies to limit the economic influence of rentiers'.

would be calculated on the basis of the international trade of each country (a 75 per cent average of imports and exports of the three years prior to the war, subject to revisions related to annual averages of world trade). This would operate through overdrafts that would make and receive payments, based on fixed, but adjustable, exchange rates. The US and United Kingdom (UK), which were hegemonic countries would control the ICU through vetoes on decisions of the governing boards.

The ICU rested on the assumption that trade balances required to be counterbalanced, with surplus countries obliged to pay a 1 per cent interest rate for bank-denominated loans above 25 per cent of the quota, a 2 per cent interest rate if credits exceeded 50 per cent of the quotas and, in this case, economies were required to create favourable import conditions, which would be imposed by the ICU's governing board. And deficit countries were required to pay a 1 per cent interest rate on their debit balances if they exceeded 25 per cent of their quotas, 2 per cent interest rates if they exceeded 50 per cent of the quotas and, under these conditions, they would be required to devalue their currencies against the bancor by 5 per cent. And, if the debit balances exceeded 75 per cent of their quotas, they could be expelled from the ICU.

The critical point of this arrangement was the low rate of interest of bilateral bancor loans, which encouraged governments and institutions to grant loans outside the ICU, at higher interest rates. Under these conditions the penalties of surplus countries were neutralized by deflationary lending to debtor countries (Toporowski 2017: lecture 1).

A counter-argument was put forward at the Bretton Woods conference by Harry Dexter White, which represented the position of the US. It proposed a United and Associated Nation Stabilization Fund, also based on quotas, comprised of gold (12.5 per cent), local currency (12.5 per cent), and government financial bonds (25 per cent). Each member state could acquire with its own currency international money up to the value of its quota, while amounts above that volume needed the approval of 80 per cent of the fund member countries. This plan, unlike the Keynes proposal, contained credits to balance the current accounts of deficit countries (Skidelsky 2017) that, in return, would be followed by deflationary adjustments to obtain finance. Keynes's 'scarce currency' clause[3] was neutralized, although,

---

[3] Keynes's plan to restore a nation's trade balance with structural deficits proposed a clause known as 'scarce currency', which would deal with the problem of countries with considerable current account deficit that would eventually leave countries with no foreign currency.

incidentally, the US tried to use this clause when faced with strong current account deficits in 1970 and 2018.[4]

The limitation of the White plan is that its operations were based on scarce currency, since international payments could only be made via 'blocked accounts' (Toporowski 2017: lecture 1), which are subject to foreign exchange controls in a country that restricts the amount of its currency that can be transferred to other countries or exchanged into other currencies.The Plan also proposed fixed exchange rates, without appropriate financial instruments to assure those rates. This forced deficit countries, indebted to the Stabilization Fund, to adopt deflationary or devaluation polices to keep a stable exchange rate peg, with no economic penalties for economies with trade surpluses.

Not discussed at the Bretton Woods conference was Kalecki's and Schumacher's suggestion that proposed a multilateral agreement, based on compensatory mechanisms, founded on national currencies that would settle trade deficits and surpluses, and guarantee a system of long-term credit to finance the economic growth of backward regions (Schumacher 1943; Kalecki and Schumacher, 1943).

This proposition included long-term loans to finance chronic trade imbalances in countries with structural current account deficit, particularly in underdeveloped geographical areas that ought to undergo industrialization processes (Kalecki and Schumacher 1943 and Kalecki 1946/1990). An International Investment Board (IIB) was proposed so that developing economies would have finance to 'catch up with' developed economies. In addition, this plan established that industrialized countries' deficits, financed by long-term credits, should be spent in other developed deficit countries (Toporowski 2017: lecture 2).

There was also a scheme put forward by Schumacher. It advocated an International Clearing Arrangement, whose aim was to support world trade expansion, independent of each country's trade balance. Each nation should have a National Clearing Fund (NCF) and accept payments for imports

---

If invoked, the 'scarce currency' clause would entitle other countries to discriminate in their trade policies against the goods of the country whose currency had become scarce because of low imports relative to exports. This would imply the countries with surplus balances would be sanctioned harder than those with debit balances, i.e. the former would be prevented from hoarding their surplus and be obliged to increase their imports or reduce their exports.

[4] The US tried in the 1970s to invoke the scarce currency clause without achieving its objective, which was raised again in the Trump period under the compensated free trade clause, where the US would set a cap on its trade deficit and impose limits on the surpluses of its business partners (see Skidelsky 2017).

and exports in the currencies of each country. The international compensation fund established assets and liabilities, in which deficit countries would accumulate stocks on national currency, while surplus countries would accumulate rights (claims) on deficit countries. This implies that the International Clearing Office (ICO) acts as owner, which is a 'Trustee in the pooling of uncleared balances. All cash balances are considered, at any time, to be taken over by the ICO, and the clearing funds of the surplus countries are considered to own a share in the Pool, equal to the size of their respective surpluses' (Schumacher 1943, cited in Toporowski 2017). And, exchange rates ought to be the result of cooperative agreements led by the NCF, which means they must be agreed by all clearing fund members 'in order that they will actually make their disbursements to their respective home exporters at the new rates' (Toporowski 2017).

The advantage of this arrangement would be that the ICO would not require its own finance, or a new international currency, since every national currency acts as a means of payment abroad. In addition, surplus countries do not have incentives to maintain that condition because

> the holding of [accumulated] surpluses becomes unprofitable and risky. The surplus, instead of being convertible into gold or interest-earning investments, is tied up in the pool: it is a share in the Pool. And the Pool's assets are always the weakest currencies of the world: the currencies of the countries that have been unable to earn as much as they have spent.
>
> (Toporowski 2017)

This proposal moved away from the equilibria assumptions and operated under the assumption that current import surpluses should be replaced by future export surpluses. It should be added that this proposal is nearer to Keynes's plan, with addition of the International Investment Board. Another characteristic of this plan is that the existence of private capital would be acknowledged, since the clearing funds not only considered payments for goods and services, patents and copyrights, but also dividends, interest, and amortization payments (Schumacher 1943: 150).

The results of the Bretton Woods conference were the adoption of an international system based on the winning country proposal (i.e. the White plan) that faced a very rapid crisis (1947) because not enough international liquidity was provided. This was solved by the adoption of the US dollar as an international unit of account. For this institutional arrangement to work the US was required to run external current account and public deficits, justified by the Cold War (aid to allied countries, opposed to the Soviet Union bloc) accompanied by a series of US military adventures. This arrangement remained tied to gold, at a price of US$35 per ounce of gold (constant over the period) which, although it was more flexible than the 'gold-standard' because only central banks could demand dollars for gold, remained tied to a 'scarce' commodity. This arrangement permitted sufficient international reserves for international trade to take place but, as said above, at the expense of enormous current account deficits of the hegemonic country (the US).

The Bretton Woods system failed to reduce structural trade imbalances among developed nations, and developing countries. In this context, the US strengthened its position as the 'hegemon' on the basis of 'exorbitant privileges'.[5] These privileges meant that the hegemonic country

> can pre-empt the world output, structurally coming first in the pecking order, with everybody else dividing among themselves what is left—the issuer of the world currency can run deficits as big as it finds fit to, and the rest of the world will just have to run as big a surplus, its resources being pre-empted by the centre country.
>
> (De Cecco 2012)

This laid the foundations of a global international financial market, subject to great speculation.

5.3 Gold Demonetization and Institutional Changes

The restrictions on international short-term private capital movements had a short life. The Eurodollar market (later known as Eurocurrency) operated as an international market, based on private capital flows. Funds in developed countries (principally in the US) activated this offshore capital market, and it was prone to financial speculation. Operation of this market commenced at the beginning of the 1950s, when European economies' currencies regained convertibility, without achieving balanced trade, or having corrective measures to reduce their imbalances. The imposition of the dollar as the unit of international exchange, together with growing structural

---

[5] The term "*exhorbitant* privileges" was proposed by Rueff in the mid-1960s in the light of financial capital dominance over productive capital, in which the privileges of the centre were considered the results 'of a higher return on its external assets than that on its external liabilities' De Cecco 2012.

trade imbalances within developed and with developing countries, was the beginning of the end of private short-term capital regulation and of fixed exchange rate structures.

The Eurodollar market had the peculiarity of being a space free from any domestic jurisdiction and was dominated by US dollar deposits. Offshore financial institutions' operations in the European market (operated mostly in London) were tolerated by economies with large financial centres (US and UK, but also Switzerland and Singapore) in the context of the Cold War initiated at the end of WWII. Financial and non-financial corporations channelled their excess reserves to the Eurodollar market.

The reasons for the expansion of the Eurodollar market were various. The first has a political nature, related to the possibility of freezing US financial assets in banks operating in the Soviet bloc in the event of a break with the western bloc (Eatwell and Taylor 2000: 36–8). Second, there is an institutional argument, in the light of the 'Interest Equalization Rate' (1964–73) that increased costs to banks of lending offshore from subsidiaries in the US, causing foreign corporations to move their deposits from US institutions to Eurobanks. This mostly occurred in the context of the industrial recession of developed countries (Eatwell and Taylor 2000: 36–8). Third, the Eurodollar market strengthened due to large inflows of capital from the surpluses of countries in the Organization of Petroleum Exporting Countries (OPEC) after the first oil shock in 1973–74. The surpluses that could not be absorbed by developed economies were recycled to middle-income oil-importing countries.

During 1970, under this international scheme a high volume of loans was granted to Latin America, based on a sustained positive commercial term of trade. The capital flows due to private credits granted by the Euromarkets increased the external debt of these economies. This was the antecedent of the region's external debt crisis, ignited by the rise in interest rates in the US in 1979. The rise caused the Mexican crisis (1982), replicated in many developing economies. In Latin America, it marked the beginning of capital deregulation, followed by deep processes of globalization and internationalization.

An important contributory factor to the demise of the Bretton Woods system was the end of dollar–gold convertibility. On 15 August 1971, President Nixon announced that the US did not have sufficient gold reserves to convert the dollars accumulated in other central banks (mainly European) into gold, declaring the end of the convertibility of gold at the Bretton Woods parity of US$35 per fine ounce. The growing mobility of international money towards the Eurodollar market[6] and the termination of dollar–gold convertibility marked the end of the international financial system agreed at the Bretton Woods conference. The fixed exchange rate structure was eliminated and interest rates became volatile, retaining the US dollar position of international unit of account, with the particularity that access to dollars took place on the basis of local private debts' (bank deposits) convertibility into debts denominated in dollars.

Flexible exchange rates and volatile interest rates transferred the risks of capital movement from the public to the private sector (Eatwell and Taylor 2000) setting the conditions for the financial system to operate at a global level. In the Bretton Woods system the risk of these exchange rate movements was borne by governments. After the downfall of the Bretton Woods system, that risk was transferred to the private sector, which became the main debtors of the economy. This gave way to a globalization setting that also activated the currency exchange market, which in the 2000s opened up and internationalized. Under this new condition, Foreign Direct Investment (FDI) and Foreign Portfolio Investment (FPI) (including short-term bank capital flows)[7] turned into the main creators of liquidity, backed by international commercial financial institutions that, on the whole, triggered the exchange currency market, as well as financial innovation.

Forms of finance changed in the light of flexible exchange rates and flexible interest rates due to private capital mobility that also involved different currencies. Financial instruments, characterized as financial innovations, were created to advance liquidity and reduce risks, giving way to complex financial relations in large financial and non-financial corporations. Debts increased as corporations expanded their balance sheets in order to reduce risks and access international units of account, i.e. foreign currency. The problem was that these institutions also promoted strong speculative activity. Thus, financial innovation become a way of appropriating profits in the financial market (financial gains) that redistributed profits in favour of large corporations, whose counterpart was the reduction of the wage share in income and jobs quality.

---

[6] Eatwell and Taylor report: 'Net Eurocurrency deposit liabilities amounted to around $10 billion in the mid-1960s and grew to $500 billion by 1980 in the industrial countries, bank deposits in currencies other than each nation's own currency amounted to one-quarter of the total' (Eatwell and Taylor 2000: 37).
[7] It is difficult to differentiate between direct and portfolio foreign investment, while the purchase of fixed assets above 10% of the total assets of a company, independent of expanding from adding gross fixed capital investment, is constituted as direct foreign investment.

In this context, financial markets deepened and broadened, giving a capital market base to financial operations. A principal feature of the post-Bretton Woods financial system was the increasing divorce between liquidity and productive activity, in the light of expanding financial innovation, which modified the operations of different institutions and economic agents. On the one hand, banks ceased to be the main providers of finance for non-financial corporations, making those corporations the main lenders of the financial system, expressed by the increased volume of treasury activities in which they engaged (Seccareccia 2012/2013). On the other hand, households became users of financial services to finance their consumption. Investment banks acquired great relevance by collecting family savings in return for insurance to guarantee services such as education, health, and pensions previously provided by the public sector. This situation generated excess net liquidity in the financial markets, creating processes of financial inflation that were unsustainable, followed by crisis, led by deflationary processes.

Additionally, productive and, especially financial, activities were internationalized in global value chains and the multinational financial entities, which transcended national geographic boundaries, displaying large cross-border movements of capital,[8] based on different underlying assets (national currencies, shares, bonds, prices, commodities). The institutional arrangement super-charged private debts, whose risks in cases of default are assumed by governments.

The great limitation of the post-war international financial system, resulting from the Bretton Woods agreements, was the imposition of fixed but adjustable exchange rates that were supposed to restore current account balances via devaluation (but only under conditions of export and import elasticity above unity). The current account deficit of the US gave life to financial markets that, in turn, gave way to globalized and complex financial relations, which restructured the post-war world monetary order. However, the immense volume of private capital mobility, along with the demonetization of gold, arose from deep and broad financial markets that incubated the seed of systemic crises in emerging market countries (in the 1990s) and the financial crisis of developed countries (in 2008).

---

[8] The volume of monetary aggregates ceased to be a variable subject to central bank control, being replaced by the rate of interest settings. Gerald Bouey (former Governor of the Banque du Canada, the central bank of Canada) answering to the monetarist complaint that central bankers excluded monetary aggregates from their control stated 'we didn't abandon the monetary aggregates, they abandoned us' Blinder 1998: 27–8.

5.4 The International Financial System and Debt in Latin America

There is an important controversy around the role of debt in the context of the global financial system that becomes more complicated if related to economic growth. On a theoretical basis, debt is an inherent element of a capitalist economic system, but it also generates economic instability.[9] In open economies, the ratio of debt to production rose exponentially because of the dominant institutional arrangements, built on different currencies which, in conjunction with flexible interest rates, exchange rates, and other prices along with credits, generated huge mobility of capital to acquire financial instruments that, instead of reducing risks, are moved by the expectation of financial gain.

Additionally, there is an apparent contradiction in the exchange rate that should be applied to economies with increasing debt (private and public) and current account deficits. Highly indebted economies benefit from overvalued exchange rates, while current account deficit countries prefer undervalued exchange rates (so long as imports and exports are elastic with respect to exchange rate flexibility, a condition that does not apply to developing countries Prebisch 1949 [1998]). Moreover, the exchange rate is an important factor in determining the price level in open economies. In conditions of globalization, stable exchange rates became the main objective of central bank monetary policies. This explains the combination of high margins of interest rates with respect to developed economies and stable (overvalued) exchange rates.

The main antecedent of the Latin American globalization process took place in the late 1980s, which led to deep debt crises, solved through the Brady Plan, which created a complex set of financial instruments to return Latin American economies to international markets.[10] This led to even wider

---

[9] From this idea, Keynes (1930, pp. 196-197) points out that banks are the institutions responsible for moving from one stage of production to another, which contrasts with the theory of liquidity preference (Keynes 1936). Minsky (1986) proposes the Financial Instability Hypothesis in place of the Preference Theory, pointing out that crises are an endogenous phenomenon generated by the indebtedness of companies, while Toporowski (2013) states that they are complex relations of the capitalist system and a function of the dominant institutional arrangements.

[10] The main financial instruments were the Par bonds that were issued at the same value as the original loan, but the coupon on the bonds is below market rate; principal and interest payments are usually guaranteed. An important role was played by the Discount bonds that were issued at a discount on the original value of the loan, but the coupon is at market rate; principal and interest payments are usually guaranteed. Other, less common, financial

access to international money through the convertibility of private local debt into private debts denominated in dollars.

5.5 A Glance at Latin American External Debt Movements

The first antecedent of the Latin American financial globalization process is the commercial openness that began with the collapse of the Import Substitution Industrialization (ISI) policy model, that gave a big boost to exports not overcoming the structural current account deficit, with some temporal exceptions (the current account was in surplus, on average, in the first five years of the 1990s in Brazil, Colombia, and, in the first decade of the twenty-first century in Argentina, Chile, and Brazil, the latter explained in terms of the positive commercial terms of trade of the period. Levy 2014).

The combination of growing exports and current account deficit forced Latin American economies to open their financial accounts and globalize their monetary systems in relatively short periods and to an extent that was rapid and profound. This process began in 1990, with accelerated inflows of external liabilities, via foreign investment (direct and portfolio), well above the needs of the domestic current account deficits in each country. This was backed by international rating agencies that did not encourage the development of domestic financial systems of these economies and directed international flows to certain activities and corporations through the issuance of investment grades.

However, the capital inflows are well above the financing needs of the current account in trade and income commitments and show. There is a high reliance on short terms capital, even within foreign direct investments, contributing to the financial instability of these countries. The excess of capital inflows over the current account deficit had been noticeable in Brazil, Chile, and Peru since 2000 (see Table 5.1a). This resulted in an excess of liquidity in international currency, particularly after the 2008 global financial crisis.

---

instruments were front-loaded interest-reduction bonds (FLIRB), new-money bonds, debt-conversion bonds (DCB), and past-due interest bonds (PDI). The Brady Bond negotiations generally involved some form of 'haircut' (the bonds resulting from restructuring were less than the face value of the claims before restructuring). Guarantees attached to Brady bonds included collateral to guarantee the principal, rolling interest guarantees, and value recovery rights. Not all Brady bonds would necessarily have all those forms of guarantee, and the specifics would vary from issuance to issuance.

Table 5.1a The Ratio of Total Financial inflows to Current Account Balance

	1980–89	1990–99	2000–09	2010/17
Argentina	0.2	−2.4	0.4	−2.1
Brazil	0.3	−1.3	−6.9	−2.2
Chile	0.0	−3.3	9.7	−5.9
Colombia	−1.4	−1.8	−2.9	−2.0
Mexico	−2.0	−1.4	−2.7	−3.7
Peru	0.4	−0.8	−7.6	−2.2

Source: Author's elaboration based on International Monetary Fund, Balance of Payments Statistics data. Available at http://data.imf.org/regular.aspx?key=61468205, accesed January 2020.

The table shows gross financial inflows related to the current account deficit (in net terms) to show that Latin American economies underwent a process of extreme financial openness and they follow monetary policies to attract foreign capital well above the needs to finance the current account deficits. Because of the short term composition of financial inflows, including foreign direct investment, (by definition the owner of 10% or more of a company's capital is defined as direct investment - see IMF's Balance of Payment Manual definition) made these economies especially vulnerable to financial instability.

The relation between external debt stocks (EDS) and gross domestic product (GDP) in the 1980s, was as expected relatively high because of the region's external debt crisis (see Table 5.1b). This coefficient drastically shrank in the 1990s in the Latin American financial crisis that took place between 1994 and the end of that decade. Following the 2008 crisis in the US, private sector debt stocks increased further in relation to GDP.

In particular, the 1995 financial crisis of Latin American countries explains the uptick of EDS in relation to GDP in the second five years of the 1990s of the last century, followed by a decline in the first decade of the twenty-first century. Finally, in the second decade of the twenty-first century the EDS/GDP ratio rose, with the inflow of excess liquidity from the US to Latin American financial markets in search of higher returns. Positive margins of interest rates in the region over rates in developed economies were offered by apparently risk free public bonds, and stable exchange rate policies that guarantee the purchasing power of external financial capital.

Table 5.1b Ratio of External debt stocks to GDP (%)

	1980–79	1990–94	1995–99	2000–04	2005–09	2010–14	2015–18
Argentina	53.0	33.1	44.8	98.3	47.0	27.7	38.6
Brazil	38.5	27.8	26.7	39.8	17.6	18.3	29.2
Colombia	35.6	31.6	32.4	35.6	22.7	23.8	40.9
Mexico	51.2	32.1	34.6	21.4	19.0	28.5	37.7
Peru	74.4	64.3	55.1	52.0	32.6	30.4	33.4
Chile*	79.0	44.2	37.8	52.2	36.1	46.6	65.0

* The data for Chile is based on CEPALSTAT. Available at https://cepalstat- prod.cepal.org/
cepalstat/tabulador/ConsultaIntegrada.asp? idIndicador=861&idioma=e, accessed 10
November 2021.

At the country level, Chile has the highest external debt (especially following the 2010 crisis) explained by the wide financial opening of this economy
(Levy 2014), the complexity of its financial relations (Pérez-Caldentey and
Favreau-Negront 2019), along with capital exports from Chile to the rest of
the world. Argentina is another highly indebted economy, but this needs
to be understood within the context of thevarious economic crises undergone by this economy in the 1980s, 1990s, and 2000s, including the 2015
crisis that occurred with the advent of President Macri. Another economy
that stands out for its high indebtedness is Peru, explained by the drastic external opening that occurred in the twenty-first century, with the
growth of its commodity exports, led by FDI in the mining sector. Colombia,
Mexico, and Brazil are the least indebted economies, explained by their stabilization policies and higher economic growth, respectively, and also lower
financial complexity, highlighting that Brazil and Mexico have the broad-
est and deepest foreign exchange centres of the region, which guarantees
access to international liquidity and better debt renegotiating possibilities
(Levy 2018).

Following the logic of the financial relations complexity, we find that the
ratio of private debt to GDP grew significantly, from the second half of the
1990s in Brazil and Peru, and to a lesser extent in Mexico (see Figure 5.1a)
and peaked by the 2000s. This can be explained by the withdrawal of public
sector direct intervention in economic activity, and the increasing liquidity requirements of the private sector in order to maintain balance sheet
equilibria, particularly notorious in the Chilean case (Perez Caldentey and
Favreau-Negront 2019). The 2008 crisis increased total liabilities, due to

excess net financial flows resulting from the quantitative easing polices of developed economies and moving in search of higher returns. These loose monetary policies made Latin America the financial recipient of external flows unrelated to its productive system.

The obvious consequence of these developments is that the public and publicly guaranteed debt ratio had been reducing, relative to GDP (see Figure 5.1b) since the 1980s, albeit delayed in Peru, less pronounced in Brazil, and relatively constant for Colombia. It should be highlighted that the Mexican economy had been rebounding at a ratio of public debt to GDP, since the 2010s. This can be explained by private sector borrowing due to the developed quantitative easing policies that directed net excess foreign capital to developing countries in search of financial returns. This was especially pronounced in Mexico due to its deep foreign exchange market.

An additional element is that the ratio of short-term debt to total external debt of the countries analysed (information for Chile is unavailable) had also been declining since 1970 (with lagged behaviour for Peru), augmenting temporarily in the second five-year period of the last decade of the twentieth century and after the 2008 crisis (with the exception of Argentina). This is shown in Table 5.1c. This indicates that the reduced weight of short-term debt of the total external debt, in turn, lowers Latin American instability.

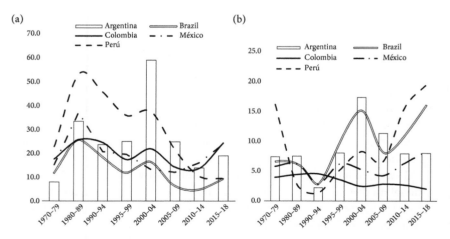

Fig. 5.1 (a) External debt stocks, public and publicly guaranteed (b) External debt stocks, private non-guaranteed % of GDP

Source: Author elaboration on World Bank data, available at https://databank.worldbank.org/source/international-debt-statisticsbased on data available

Table 5.1c Short-term debt (% of total external debt)

	1970–79	1980–79	1990–94	1995–99	2000–04	2005–09	2010–14	2015–18
Argentina	88.3	217.7	118.3	126.3	136.9	67.3	74.7	135.5
Brazil	59.0	190.6	159.8	66.9	66.4	25.1	13.7	15.6
Colombia	162.1	71.2	37.6	60.6	33.6	26.6	28.1	27.4
Mexico	167.1	313.6	232.0	125.3	40.7	29.3	42.9	33.6
Peru	7.4	6.9	3.9	4.7	5.0	6.2	3.6	4.0

Table 5.1d Total reserves as % of total external debt

	1970–79	1980–79	1990–994	1995–99	2000–04	2005–09	2010–14	2015–18
Argentina	24.7	10.7	16.7	17.3	10.7	31.7	29.1	20.5
Brazil	24.0	8.0	16.4	24.9	18.1	61.4	78.6	67.2
Colombia	30.3	35.8	38.1	29.5	30.2	45.0	44.5	37.7
Mexico	10.4	6.8	13.3	16.2	31.7	46.5	47.3	40.6
Peru	12.5	15.8	17.1	33.4	34.1	74.5	102.6	91.3

Source: Author's elaboration based on World Bank data. Aavailable at https://databank.
worldbank.org/source/international-debt-statistics, accessed 16 January 2020.

The large cost of increased openness of Latin American economies (and emerging markets in general) is the magnitude of reserves to total debt (Table 5.1d). With the exception of Argentina, we found that the countries analysed showed a considerable increase in this ratio, particularly in Peru, Mexico, and Brazil, which implies keeping high volumes of idle international currency liquidity, that is costly for economies in terms of interest income.

Finally, in terms of institutions issuing outstanding debts in the international market, in general governments take the lead, showing a downward trend (with the exception of Argentina), followed in importance by financial institutions and non-financial institutions since the process of the internationalization of the financial system initiated in the 2000s (see Table 5.2). At the domestic level, the same pecking order takes place, highlighting the undeveloped character of financial operations taking place at the domestic level.

Table 5.2 Debt securities issues and amount outstanding in the international and domestic markets by country, in relation to their GDP (%)

Argentina	1990–99	2000–09	2010–17	Brasil	1990–99	2000–09	2010–17
International Market				**International Market**			
Financial Corporations	9.0	4.8	23.7	Financial Corporations	19.8	17.5	36.8
Non-financial Corporations	26.2	9.5	0.0	Non-financial Corporations	23.7	15.4	24.3
General government	72.0	85.6	76.3	General government	54.1	67.1	38.9
Domestic Market				**Domestic Market**			
Financial Corporations		89.3	23.7	Financial Corporations		20.6	27.8
Non-financial Corporations		0.0	0.0	Non-financial Corporations		3.4	6.4
General government		10.7	76.3	General government		76.0	65.7

Continued

Table 5.2 *Continued*

Colombia	1990–99	2000–09	2010–17
International Market			
Financial Corporations	8.1	5.1	10.8
Non-financial Corporations	19.0	28.0	55.3
General goverment	72.3	66.9	34.0
Domestic Market			
Financial Corporations		28.7	29.9
Non-financial Corporations		10.2	8.0
General goverment		61.0	62.1

Mexico	2000–09	2010–17
International Market		
Financial Corporations	2.9	16.0
Non-financial Corporations	6.9	24.0
General goverment	90.2	60.0
Domestic Market		
Financial Corporations	0.0	0.0
Non-financial Corporations	1.6	2.2
General goverment	98.4	97.8

Peru	1993–99	2000–09	2010–17
International Market			
Financial markets	34.4	7.5	29.1
Non-financial Corporations	24.2	3.1	20.2
General goverment	47.2	89.5	50.7
Domestic Market			
Financial Corporations		43.1	36.0
Non-financial Corporations		21.5	14.6
General goverment		35.4	49.4

Source: Author's calculations based on data from the Bank of International Settlements. Available at https://stats.bis.org/statx/srs/table/c1, accessed 16 January 2020.

5.6 Conclusions

Capital account opening in developing countries with current account structural deficits proved to be a process of globalization and financial complexity, dominated by private capital movements, which provided liquidity in international units of account. The ratio of liquidity to production expanded with unusual rapidity because it made finance available to settle debts, denominated in the international account unit (dollars), as well as providing liquidity for the foreign exchange market, and backing the dollar note circulation in domestic economies and reserves in foreign currency.

Additionally, these institutional rearrangements modified the amount and composition of debts: they were directed by private capital that resulted in an increased volume of the debts of developing economies (the 1980s external debt crises and the 1990s emerging market crises). This indicates that the institutional organization imposed in this period came along with expansionary cycles with high liquidity, followed by cycles of increased debts and illiquidity. The peculiarity of Latin America economies is that, after the process of globalization, which resulted in a deep financial crisis (mid-1990s), liquidity in international denominated units of account drastically increased, but it took place at the expense of lower degrees of economic policy autonomy.

The need to guarantee liquidity for international trade and economic development has been a constant, unresolved, concern for the designers of international financial systems. The Bretton Woods system was unsuccessful because international liquidity depended on the US trade deficit, which generated deep structural problems to this economy, and laid the foundations of an offshore financial market that became the prelude to economic globalization and financial complexity in large corporations. This gave way to an era of growing trade imbalances, accompanied by an important expansion of activity in capital markets which, along with higher liquidity, led to practices of financial innovation (speculation), which severely limited economic development, especially in emerging countries with structural deficits of current accounts.

Comparative studies of financial development between Latin America and South East Asia (Stallings and Studart 2006) show that the financial opening in Latin America was deeper and faster than in South East Asia, with slower development in its financial markets. This implied that the deepening of the financial markets of Latin America was less deep and more restricted and relatively detached from the production process. Foreign direct investment was not linked to local capital markets, and foreign portfolio investment remained in government securities that accrue financial gains for large transnational capital, on the basis of proportionally high interest rates and stable exchange rates that together limited bonds and share markets in Latin American economies.

The transformation of the Latin American financial system was profound. Initially it was as a result of the breakdown of the import-substitution model, to the great disadvantage of governments of the region obliged to prioritize economic stability (low inflation) and direct economic development over export-led growth to make domestic economic growth sustainable. Latin American economies opted for commercial, productive, and financial openness, and an intense insertion of the region's economies into the international market, in exchange for access to international liquidity access that, however, remained subject to decisions of the international sphere.

Acknowledgement

The author acknowledges support the support for the research in this chapter from DGAPA-UNAM under Research Project IN -306120.

References

Amsden, Alice 2004 'La sustitución de importaciones en la industria de alta tecnología. Prebisch renace en Asia' (Import substitution in high-tech industries: Prebisch lives in Asia), *Revista CEPAL* 82(April): 75–90.

Blinder, Alan S. 1998 *Central Banking in Theory and Practice.* Cambridge, MA: MIT Press.

Borio, Claudio and Piti Disyatat 2015 'Capital flows and the current account. Taking financing (more) seriously', BIS, Working Paper 525, October. Basle

De Cecco, Marcello 2012 'Global Imbalances: Past, Present, and Future', *Contributions to Political Economy* 31: 29–50.

Eatwell, John and Lance Taylor 2000 *Global Finance at Risk.* New York: The New Press.

Kalecki, Michał 1946 [1990] 'Multilateralism and Full Employment', in Jerzy Osiatyński (ed.) *Collected Works of Michal Kalecki Volume I Capitalism: Business Cycles and Full Employment.* Oxford: Clarendon Press pp. 409–416.

Kalecki, M. And Schumacher, E.F. (1943) 'International Clearing and Long-Term Lending' *Bulletin of the Institute of Statistics Oxford Supplement No. 5*

Volume 5, 7 August, pp. 29-33 in J. Osiatyński (ed.) *Collected Works of Michał Kalecki Volume VII Studies in Applied Economics 1940-1967 Miscellanea* Oxford: The Clarendon Press 1997.

Keynes, John Maynard, 1930 *The Collected Writings of John Maynard Keynes Volume VI A Treatise on Money 2 The Applied Theory of Money* London and Basingstoke, Macmillan for the Royal Economic Society 1971.

Keynes, John Maynard 1936 [1964] *The General Theory of Employment Interest, and Money.* London: Macmillan.

Levy, Noemi 2014 'Latin America in the New International Order: New Forms of Economic Organizations and Old Form of Surplus Appropriation', in Noemi Levy and Etelberto Ortiz (eds) *The Financialisation Response to Economic Disequilibria. European and Latin American Experiences.* Cheltenham: Edward Elgar, pp. 90–107.

Levy, Noemi (2018) 'The Internationalization of Local Currencies of Emerging Countries: The Experience of the Mexican Peso and the Chinese Renminbi', *Brazilian Keynesian Review.* 4(1): 14–34.

Minsky, Hyman P. 1986 *Stabilizing an Unstable Economy.* New Haven, CT: Yale University Press.

Perez-Caldentey, Esteban and Nicole Favreau-Negront 2019 'Financialisation in a Small Open Developing Economy: The Case of Chile', in Noemi Levy and Jorge Bustamante (eds) *Financialisation in Latin America. Challenges of the Export–Led Growth Model.* Abingdon: Routledge, pp. 179–98.

Prebisch, Raúl 1949 [1998] 'El desarrollo económico en América Latina y algunos de sus principales problemas' (Some principal problems in the economic development of Latin America), in Ricardo Bielschowsky (ed.) *Cincuenta años pensamiento en la CEPAL, Texto seleccionados* (Fifty years of CEPAL ideas). FCE-CEPAL, pp. 69–129.

Rodrik, Dani 2010 'Greek Lessons for the World Economy' Project Syndicate. Available at https://www.project-syndicate.org/commentary/greek-lessons-for-the-world-economy?barrier=accesspaylog, accessed 10 November 2021.

Russell, Ellen D. 2008 *New Deal Banking Reforms and Keynesian Welfare Capitalism.* London and New York: Routledge.

Schumacher, Ernst F. 1943 'Multilateral Clearing', *Economica* New Series, 10(38): May, pp. 150–165.

Seccareccia, Mario 2012/2013. 'Financialization and the Transformation of Commercial Banking: Understanding the Recent Canadian Experience before and during the International Financial Crisis', *Journal of Post Keynesian Economics* 35(2): 277–300.

Skidelsky, Robert 2017 'Resurrecting Creditor Adjustment' *Project Syndicate*, October. https://www.project-syndicate.org/commentary/scarce-currency-clause-trade-imbalances-by-robert-skidelsky-2017-10

Stalling, Barbara and Rogerio Studart 2006 *Finance for Development. Latin America in Comparative Perspectives.* United Nations, ECLAC: Brookings Institution Press.

Taylor, John B. 1993 'Discretion vs Policy Rules in Practice', *Carnegie-Rochester Conference Series on Public Policy* 39(December): 195–214.

Toporowski, Jan 2013 'El neologismo como una innovación en la economía: el caso de la Financiarización' (Neologism as theoretical innovation in economics: the case of financialization), in Noemi Levy and Tereza López (eds) *Financiariazación y modelo de acumulación. Aportes de países en desarrollo* (Financialization and the model of accumulation in developing countries). Mexico City: Facultad De Economía, Unam, pp. 31–46.

Toporowski, Jan 2017 'Credit and Finance in International Monetary Theory', *Lectures of Jan Toporowski*, UNAM, Mexico.

6

Long-Term Investment and its Financing

The Role of Development Banks

Stephany Griffith-Jones

In memory of the late Julio Lopez, from whom I first learned, and learned so well, about Michael Kalecki.

6.1 Introduction and the Significance of Kalecki's Thinking

In the context of the Kaleckian and Keynesian traditions, level of investment is a key determinant not just of output, and future output, as well as the future evolution of productivity, but also very significantly of the level of savings. As a consequence, ensuring sufficient levels of investment is key for developed economies, but especially for emerging and developing ones.

One of the key constraints for ensuring sufficient levels of investment, and channelling it to the most productive sectors of the economy or those whose productivity is likely to increase most, is lack of sufficient levels of long-term financing. One effective way in which such finance is and can be mobilized is via national development banks (NDBs).

Turning to the analysis of development banks, I would like to explore more the current economic context, and the need to adjust the Kalecki theoretical framework to this new reality in the dynamics of an economy where financial markets dominate over investment into expansion of real capital assets (Chapter 1 and Osiatyński 2019).

As Osiatyński (2019) clearly puts it, for Kalecki the business cycle is an inherent feature of investing in productive capital assets that takes place in the real sector of the economy. Therefore the primary cause of business fluctuations is the time lag between the income effect that appears when

Stephany Griffith-Jones, *Long-Term Investment and its Financing*. In: *International Equilibrium and Bretton Woods*. Edited by Jerzy Osiatyński and Jan Toporowski, Oxford University Press. © Oxford University Press (2022). DOI: 10.1093/oso/9780192856401.003.0007 investment is being made, and the supply effect, which appears later, once capital assets start operating. For Kalecki, business fluctuations and economic dynamics are embedded in the real sector of the economy. Financing of investment is not a separate determinant of these cyclical fluctuations.

However, the economic dynamic in today's capitalism is heavily influenced by the dynamics of the financial sector. The latter can be broadly characterized as unfettered and insufficiently regulated finance, which has a major influence on the real economy, both in its normal fluctuations, as well as ever more frequent financial crises, initially in the emerging and developing countries, but more recently also in the US and Europe.

Indeed, both Keynes and Minsky already saw the primary cause of business fluctuations in the operation of financial markets. It may well be that under present-day financial capitalism, business fluctuations, and especially financial crises are in fact determined by global financial markets and ruled by the mechanisms discussed by Minsky and Keynes rather than by those of Kalecki's thinking. Therefore the important theoretical challenge is to explain investment decisions in ways that combine Kaleckian and Minskian, as well as Keynesian, determinants of financial and business cycles and economic dynamics more generally.

This leads also, from a policy perspective, to the importance of finding ways to fund private investment that are not dependent on the vagaries of short-termist financial capital (see Section 6.2), but are based on long-term finance, as for example provided by development banks, which have also the virtue of being instruments for industrial policy, which can channel funding not just to the real economy rather than to more speculative types of activities, but also to priority sectors, such as those that form part of the green transformation.

It is important also to emphasize that national and regional development banks can play a key counter-cyclical role, from a macroeconomic perspective. For example, in the wake of the Euro-zone debt crisis, Northern European governments were reluctant to allow significant Keynesian or Kaleckian types of expansion of fiscal spending (including increased public investment) clearly needed to help boost economic recovery in the European economy, given the scale of the recession. They were, however, willing instead to engage in a sort of Keynesianism (or Kaleckianism) *sans dire*, by way of providing resources to the European Investment Bank (EIB)—the largest public multilateral bank in the world—mainly in the form of European Commission guarantees at a significant level (Griffith-Jones and Naqvi 2021). This major programme was denominated the European Fund for Strategic Investments, but was better known as the Juncker Plan. The programme was able to generate, due to leverage of private resources, up to €500 billion of finance for private investment, including in high priority sectors, during the 2015–20 period in European Union economies.

More generally, development banks (nationally, regionally, and internationally) have become major economic actors. Worldwide they have over US$11 trillion of assets; annually their loans and other transactions represent over US$2 trillion. This is equivalent to about 10 per cent of total global investment (Griffith-Jones et al. 2020a). Therefore, when sufficiently capitalized, they have the power and ability to play important counter-cyclical roles.

In some ways, these new developments relate to Kalecki and Schumacher's 1943 proposals in their paper which examined the Keynes and White plans at Bretton Woods (see Chapter 1). Kalecki and Schumacher (1943) pointed out that the formation of an international clearing organization (or fund) would not provide the rest of the world with a sufficient supply of foreign exchange from the countries which experience notorious surpluses in their balance of payments' current accounts and rising reserves of foreign exchange (or gold). To overcome this problem, Kalecki and Schumacher proposed to establish, next to the clearing union, an affiliated investment bureau whose credit activity would assure the availability of foreign exchange from countries which experience chronic export surpluses.

Chapters 3 and 8 in this volume clearly elaborate the discussion of Kalecki's and Schumacher's proposals, showing the central role they gave to public development bank financing at a multilateral level to both facilitate international equilibrium and help fund investment in developing economies. Indeed, Kalecki and Schumacher argued that:

There is no merit in a general policy aiming at *Current account equilibrium* for all countries, because different countries are at different stages of economic development, and a regular flow of investment from the more highly developed to the more backward regions of the world may redound to the benefit of all. This is implicitly recognised in both schemes [Keynes and White], since they are both to be supplemented by proposals for an International Investment Board.

Kalecki and Schumacher believed that the long-term goal of current account equilibrium in the Keynes and White plans should be abandoned, to allow governments to pursue whatever levels of aggregate demand they wish.

The authors argued therefore that currency support arrangements should be differentiated, according to whether a country has a trade deficit because it is in the process of industrialization, or because there are other reasons. They suggested an extension of the powers of the International Investment Board. This board would direct part of trade surpluses to industrializing countries. These loans were supposed to allow for the additional imports required for industrialization. In this way the weak equilibrating mechanism in the Keynes plan would be assisted by recycling the surpluses of industrialized countries through orders for industrial equipment for developing countries. These orders would generate machine exports from industrialized countries in current account deficit, while at the same time facilitating the 'unbalanced equilibrium' required in developing countries.

As Toporowski rightly highlights, Kalecki and Schumacher's argument, that countries in the process of industrialization require financing to be able to run trade deficits, was to become a feature of the development economics thinking that emerged after World War II (WWII) and is still relevant today. To the extent that these deficits corresponded to investment requiring imports, it was important that multilateral (and later also regional) development banks played a key role in funding the imports required for investment, also to avoid excessive, often expensive and too short term, borrowing from private creditors. Thus, Kalecki was arguing for a large-scale institution, providing long-term development finance, much larger than the World Bank then created, and playing a far more central role in financing long-term development. In that sense Kalecki seems very central to current discussions on enhancing the role of development banks, multilaterally, regionally, and nationally, both in terms of a much needed response to the major recessions caused by the Covid crisis and previously by the financial crisis of 2008–09; as well as being a key mechanism for funding the major investment needed to achieve a speedy and radical transformation to net zero carbon, including more inclusive economies. These issues were amply debated at a high level research conference leading to the first world summit on development banks in November 2020, under the sponsorship of President Macron and the UN Secretary General Guterrez.[1]

---

[1] Details of the research programme and conference and corresponding papers are available at https://www.afd.fr/en/actualites/agenda/visible-hand-development-banks-transition; for synthesis of the research programme, see Griffith-Jones et al. 2020a.

The rest of the paper focuses on NDBs, which are in fact much larger in their total scale than multilateral and regional ones and which play key roles in national economies.

6.2 The Role of National Development Banks

In many developed, emerging, and developing countries NDBs are central in deciding which activities should be financially supported and link them to the more general development strategies of those countries. Development banks also help avoid or moderate boom–bust cycles in external and domestic financing. By diversifying the financial system to include development banks, systemic risk may be reduced.

One basic problem of many emerging and developing countries is that their domestic financial markets are thin. In particular, they are characterized by a strong prevalence of short-term financial assets and liabilities. This means that the capacity to finance investment is limited, forcing firms to rely on short-term loans to do so, or limit their investment to what they can finance with retained profits. However, this is often limited to existing firms, and thus financial constraints limit, in particular, new activities associated with structural change. It is noteworthy that even in developed economies newer firms tend to have difficulty in raising finance, as they for example lack collateral and a track record; these problems are more acute during and after financial or other crises, for example in the current Covid crisis.

The major problems generated by these features of financial markets in terms of stability is that emerging and developing economies especially face variable mixes of maturity and currency mismatches in portfolios. This means that, during crises, creditors may refuse to roll over short-term loans, generating a liquidity crunch. Domestic bond markets—if they have developed—will face a reduction in the availability of financing, and shorter maturities and/or higher interest rates, affecting those firms still able to issue new securities. For larger firms that have borrowed abroad, debt ratios will rise if exchange rates are flexible or countries with fixed-exchange rate regimes are forced to depreciate their exchange rates to manage adverse external shocks.

Given the major limitations and stability issues that financial sectors face, development banks play an essential role from both structural transformation and stability perspectives. As extensively argued in the conclusions of a research project and book, in which I worked jointly with Jose

Antonio Ocampo (Griffith-Jones and Ocampo 2018), NDBs should have five main functions, which help cover associated market failures: (i) providing counter-cyclical financing; (ii) promoting innovation and structural transformation; (iii) supporting infrastructure investment; (iv) enhancing financial inclusion; (v) supporting the provision of public goods, particularly combating climate change.

Function (i) makes development banks an additional instrument of counter-cyclical macroeconomic policy, and (iii) makes them an instrument of infrastructure financing. Promoting small start-ups or investment in small and medium-sized enterprises linked to start-ups, as part of the broader objective of financial inclusion (iv), may be essential for structural change. And many of the activities associated with mitigating and adapting to climate change, included under (v), are innovative activities on their own. Function (ii) of development banks as promoters of innovation and structural transformation is especially important.

The failure mentioned at the start of this section, of private financial markets to deliver adequate funding in a stable manner, at sufficient maturities to fund long-term investment, and at reasonable cost in local currencies, discussed in Section 6.1, has led many governments to rely more on NDBs. The importance of these banks is a crucial feature of financial sectors in successful emerging economies like China, India, and the Republic of Korea, but also of successful developed countries, notably Germany. Several African and Asian countries recently created NDBs, and most European countries (like Portugal and Ireland) also did so, while others expanded existing ones (BPI France, for example). African countries have also started creating new NDBs, for example in Nigeria and Ghana. There seems to be a sort of renaissance of development banks!

For a long time, the topic of NDBs was largely neglected in the academic and policy literature. Since the 2007–09 North Atlantic financial crisis support for these institutions has been increasing, and this seems to be further stimulated by the Covid crisis. This has led to the need to understand key issues in relation to them: how they operate; what instruments, incentives, and governance work better; how they link to broader government policies; and importantly, how they link with private financial agents and the private sector in general, as their major objective should be to promote private investment.

In Griffith-Jones and Ocampo (2018), we analysed NDBs in seven countries (Germany, China, Brazil, Chile, Colombia, Mexico, and Peru). We conclude that overall these banks tend to be successful at what they do—with variable success associated with their relative size. They have been broadly efficient development policy instruments, helping overcome major market failures, and doing so in a flexible way over time. Furthermore, they have played important roles in funding investment for structural adjustment as part of national development strategies.

The NDBs covered in the analysis have important differences. There are countries with individual banks (Germany, Brazil, and Chile), others in which they are part of a system of NDBs with sectorial functions (Colombia and Peru), and a final group in which there is a system of NDBs but it is dominated by an individual bank (China and Mexico).

Their funding strategies vary: though having paid-in capital provided by governments, many also raise funds on national and international private capital markets, mixing in a variable way special fiscal resources channelled through them, as well as loans from multilateral and regional development banks. Leveraging public resources with private funds has been especially valued in contexts of limited fiscal space, typical during and after crises. Their instruments to provide funding also vary by country and through time. Aside from lending and equity investments in new firms, there are new instruments that are increasingly used by these institutions: guarantees, and venture capital, venture debt, and debt funds.[2]

The size of these institutions varies significantly among the countries studied (Figure 6.1). China, Germany, and Brazil have very large NDBs, with assets in the range of 15–19 per cent of GDP. In contrast, the size of NDBs is only about 2–3 per cent of GDP in Chile, Colombia, and Mexico. Peru is an intermediate case, but if we exclude the largest of its institutions (Banco de la Nación), which is really a state-owned commercial bank with some limited development functions, it belongs to the second category.

Among the functions mentioned previously, it is key to emphasize that NDBs were clearly counter-cyclical in the wake of the North Atlantic financial crisis of 2008. According to World Bank data, they increased their lending from US$1.16 trillion to US$1.58 trillion between 2007 and 2009; that is by 36 per cent; this increase in lending in hard times was far higher than the mere 10 per cent increase in private bank credit in the same countries. For Latin America, research shows that NDBs increase lending by 3.4 per cent annually in normal times and by over 10 per cent in crisis periods; private banks behaved pro-cyclically and reduce the growth of lending in crisis periods (Brei and Schlarek 2013). Preliminary information about

---

[2] For a detailed discussion, see Griffith-Jones et al. 2020b.

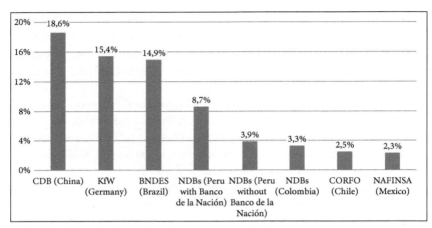

Fig. 6.1 Assets of NDBs as a proportion of GDP, 2015
Source: Bankscope and NDBs

the response to the Covid crisis shows that NDBs are again playing a key counter-cyclical role (McDonald et al. 2020).

Given the pro-cyclical nature of private finance, the counter-cyclical role of NDBs should be seen as a complement to counter-cyclical fiscal, monetary, and foreign exchange policies. Just as central banks provide key liquidity in bad times, NDBs provide crucial finance in those periods, particularly of a long-term character, to support the economic recovery and help finance and maintain investment levels, essential for not interrupting the process of structural transformation. The counter-cyclical role that NDBs play implies, of course that they should not only expand financing during crises, but also moderate it during booms.

Moreover, development banks have played a key role in fostering innovation and entrepreneurship in national economies, essential to achieving the structural transformation needed to ensure development. As Mazzucato and Penna (2018) argue, there is mounting evidence that NDBs have fostered patient, long-term, committed finance for mission-oriented investment in innovative activities. In fact, they are increasingly providing long-term committed venture capital for innovation projects. Because these projects are risky and uncertain, and nobody knows the likelihood of success, private finance shies away from supporting them, thus making the role of NDBs crucial. If successful, these projects generate positive externalities, inducing further innovation. In several cases, private investors join NDBs in the venture capital funds, with the public–private sector mix having positive features: for the private sector, the guarantee of a strong link to government policy and for the public sector the advantage of greater mobilization of resources.

KfW, originally *Kredit für Wiederaufbau*, the German development bank, for example, invests in the modernization of industries and has encouraged the development of new sectors, notably renewable energy over the past decade or so. China Development Bank (CDB), the Chinese development bank, is the largest NDB in the world. It has supported and nurtured new ventures and innovation, some of which have been behind the continued success of the Chinese economy. The Banco Nacional do Desenvolvimento Econômico e Social (National Bank for Economic and Social Development BNDES), the Brazilian development bank began to experiment with financing programmes targeted at high-tech firms and innovation development in the 1990s; it has a venture capital fund, CRIATEC, whose results are striking: in its first four years of existence, the value of the CRIATEC portfolio grew at a rate of 50 per cent per annum.

In Chile, the Corporación de Fomento de la Producción (Production Development Corporation, CORFO), the Chilean development agency, has provided long-term resources to expand the role of risk capital funds. Moreover, it created its start-up programme, which has received international recognition. This programme has encouraged the improvement and broadening of the policy mix to support these companies in Chile. For example, relevant regulations have been simplified, and financing has also been expanded to support different phases of the projects. Finally, CORFO has helped design a more detailed industrial strategy.

In Colombia, the Banco de Comercio Exterior (Bank of Foreign Trade BANCOLDEX) as a bank for trade and industrial growth in Colombia, manages a specific innovation programme, iNNpulsa Colombia. The programme supports innovation for business growth for firms of all sizes and ages, and in all sectors and regions of the country. Among its specific instruments is the national network of 'angel investors', which it co-finances, and different regional initiatives to promote the incubation and growth of firms, training in technology transfer and commercialization, and support strategies to encourage rapid business growth. As in the case of CORFO, the major problem of these programmes is their small scale.

The activities of NDBs supporting key new sectors serve as an important leverage to attract private investors. A remarkable case is renewable energy and energy efficiency. For example, KfW was initially the sole lender to private companies investing in solar energy in Germany, but later private banks followed. In China, CDB helped design broad policy to encourage investment in renewables, especially solar, as well as playing a major role in initial funding. Germany and especially China have been major actors in promoting the spread of solar energy worldwide, at increasingly competitive cost with fossil fuels. Their NDBs played a major role in catalysing this, thus contributing in a major way to climate change mitigation.

NDBs thus have developed new instruments, such as guarantees, equity—including venture capital—and debt funds. Direct loan instruments continue to be important, though greater emphasis than in the past is placed on second-tier loans (on-lending through commercial or other banks) which may make it more difficult to use NDBs as a direct instrument for industrial policy. In the area of financial inclusion, correspondent stores have been an important new instrument, which can be widely used by commercial banks.

It should be underscored that the broader context in which development banks operate is key for their success. Thus, good macroeconomic policies—in particular, active counter-cyclical policies, relatively low inflation, moderate real interest rates, and competitive and stable real exchange rates—are essential to the success of NDBs. A well-functioning financial sector is another important pre-condition for the smooth running of an effective NDB. It is also interesting to note that NDBs can help develop a deeper and better capital market. Thus, the Chinese CDB, for example, played a key role in the development of the Chinese bond market. More generally, a number of NDBs have helped the introduction of local currency and green bonds into their own local capital market.

NDBs can operate far more effectively if the country has a clear national development strategy, ideally linked to a modern industrial policy—which should focus on promoting innovative sectors and guaranteeing their competitiveness. Development banks like KfW, CDB, and CORFO operate broadly in the context of a clear strategic direction. Policy mandates are particularly valuable if they do not change too much with different governments, allowing continuity and long-term planning for the NDBs and their support for development, as the German example notably indicates.

A key question, however, is whether, given major current development challenges, NDBs do enough, especially in Latin American and African countries, but also more broadly. In particular, is their current scale large enough for the structural transformation and development needs of their countries?

In Griffith-Jones and Ocampo 2018 we show that there is a greater need for larger scale NDB activity in most Latin American countries—the major exception being, of course, Brazil, which already has a large NDB, though its size is being reduced. Preliminary evidence from Africa leads to similar conclusions. This is due to the low levels of both private and public investment. In the case of private investment, this is linked in part to the limitations of private finance, in particular its capacity to fund long-term investment associated with innovative activities. Furthermore, Latin American countries have limited fiscal space, which limits public sector investment. The leverage of public resources provided by NDBs therefore becomes particularly attractive in boosting investment.

At the same time, there is a greater need for higher investment in Latin America and Africa as the recession induced by Covid requires additional funding to support companies, and as the challenges of structural transformation become more urgent, and are linked to the need for a radically different economic model: more dynamic and smarter, with better innovation and improved ability to adapt to it, to increase productivity more rapidly; a model that is more inclusive, to reduce the large income inequalities; and—above all—a model that is greener to satisfy the urgent needs of climate change mitigation.

Furthermore, the new development model may become less reliant on international trade, which has grown more slowly than in the past since the North Atlantic financial crisis and the Covid crisis, thus turning cross-border trade into a less dynamic engine for growth. It has also been threatened by protectionist tendencies in some major developed economies, especially the US, under the Trump administration.

Uncertainty surrounds investment in new sectors and technologies, which makes such investment unlikely in most cases to be funded purely by private financial institutions, which are unwilling to take large risks, especially for long maturities. Therefore, NDBs' finance, which has the virtue of being long term (as over 50 per cent of NDB lending is for over ten years' maturity) and includes innovative activities, is needed on a significant scale.

The need for larger scale investment has been understood in the highly successful economies of Germany and China, where the scale of NDB assets, in proportion to the country's GDP is fairly large.

As a result, it seems a key conclusion that, in many emerging and developing countries the scale of operations of NDBs should be significantly increased, so they can make a more significant impact on increasing investment for structural transformation and development. This does not necessarily imply large government resources, as the only public contributions would be an increase in their paid-in capital and special programmes that governments want to promote. These NDBs could then fund their operations on the private domestic market—fairly developed in some emerging countries—as well as international capital markets. Multilateral and regional development banks, as well as international climate funds can play a key role in their financing.

Expanding the role of NDBs in countries that have them, or creating them in those that do not would therefore help to create a financial system that better serves the needs of the real economy, of society in general, and of structural transformation in particular. Indeed, the existence of a more mixed financial sector, that combines both public and private institutions in a creative and efficient way, may be a new paradigm for funding structural transformation in the twenty-first century.

It is important to underscore, finally, that what should be promoted are 'good' development banks. This implies having institutions with clear mandates, a good governance structure, and are well managed, so they fulfil their functions well. As pointed out, they should also be inserted into a clear national development strategy and supported by adequate macroeconomic policies. Their main objective is to maximize their development impact rather than profits, though assuring at least minimal returns.

6.3 Conclusions

This chapter started by showing the relevance of Kaleckian (and Keynesian) thinking to the analysis of development banks. Kalecki showed the centrality of ensuring appropriate levels of investment in determining output, future output, and savings. The imperfections of private financial markets imply the need for a mixed economy approach to finance, which ensures sufficient funding for private investment, especially in sectors with high priority for future development. Here, NDBs can play a key role. Kalecki also added a valuable international dimension in emphasizing the need for public development banks at a multilateral level providing sufficient loans to help finance imports by emerging and developing countries from developed economies, as well as from current account surplus economies. In many ways, suitably adapted to the changing world economy, this is as relevant today as it was when Kalecki was writing.

This chapter has emphasized two crucial links between finance and structural change. The first one is a direct contribution to supporting innovative sectors with long-term funding, also known as patient capital. In this regard, we have highlighted the role of NDBs linked to strong development policies, which place structural change at the centre of economic strategy, and with adequate support from macroeconomic policies. The support of innovation with long-term financing is complementary to other functions of these institutions, including supporting the provision of public goods, particularly through financing infrastructure and investments that help combat climate change; and through financial inclusion, particularly through the backing of small start-up firms and small and medium-sized businesses linked to innovative sectors. NDBs can do this task through their own first- and second-tier lending, but also through additional instruments, particularly guarantees, venture capital, and debt funds. In all cases, NDBs should not supplant private financing but rather complement and leverage additional private funds for innovative activities.

The second aspect that we emphasize is avoiding the risks associated with boom–bust cycles in domestic private financing. At the domestic level, avoiding unsustainable credit booms, and managing the maturity and currency mismatches in portfolios and the deficiencies of futures markets, when they exist, is important. NDBs should also be active in the provision of counter-cyclical financing during economic recessions, to help maintain investment levels, so as to support economic activity and employment in the short term, as well as sustainable and equitable development in the long term.

References

Brei, M., Schclarek, A., 2013 'Public Bank Lending in Times of Crisis' *Journal of Financial Stability* 9, 820–830.

Griffith-Jones, Stephany and Natalya Naqvi 2021 'Leveraging Policy Steer? Industrial Policy, Risk-Sharing and the European Investment Bank', in D. Mertens, M. Thiemann, and P. Volberding (eds) *The Reinvention of Development Banking in the European Union*. Oxford: Oxford University Press, pp. 90–114.

Griffith-Jones, Stephany and José Antonio Ocampo (eds) 2018 *The Future of National Development Banks*. Oxford, New York: Oxford University Press.

Griffith-Jones, Stephany, Régis Marodon, José Antonio Ocampo, and Jiajun Xu 2020a '10 policy recommendations for decision makers on Public Development Banks', available at https://www.afd.fr/sites/afd/files/2020-11-02-21-10/SynthesePapiersdeRecherche_PDBs_FR.pdf.

Griffith-Jones, Stephany, Shari Spiegel, Jiajun Xu, Marco Carreras, and Natalya Naqvi 2020b 'Matching risks with instruments in development banks&#x201D'. *Working Paper* 170. Paris: Agence Française de Dévelopment, available at https://www.afd.fr/en/ressources/matching-risks-instruments-development-banks.

Kalecki, Michał and Ernst F. Schumacher 1943 'International Clearing and Long-Term Lending', in Jerzy Osiatyński (ed.) *Collected Works of Michał Kalecki Volume VII Studies in Applied Economics 1940–1967 Miscellanea.* Oxford: Clarendon Press. pp. 226–232.

McDonald, David A., Thomas Marois, and Diana Barrowclough (eds) 2020 *Public Banks and Covid-19 Combatting the Pandemic with Public Finance.* Kingston, Geneva, Brussels: Municipal Services Projects, UNCTAD, and Eurodad.

Mazzucato, Mariana. and Caetano Penna 2018 'National Development Banks and Mission Oriented Finance for Innovation', in Stephany Griffith-Jones and José Antonio Ocampo (eds) *The Future of National Development Banks.* Oxford, New York: Oxford University Press. pp. 255–277.

Osiatyński, Jerzy 2019 'Kazimierz Łaski's *Lectures in Macroeconomics* under Financial Capitalism', *European Journal of Economics and Economic Policies: Intervention* 16(3, Dec): 302–17.

Toporowski, Jan 2018 *Michał Kalecki: An Intellectual Biography, Volume 2: By Intellect Alone 1939–1970.* Basingstoke: Palgrave.

7

Do We Need a New Bretton Woods to Tackle the Crisis of Modern Capitalism?

Julio López Gallardo and Hanna Szymborska

7.1 Introduction

Establishing the Bretton Woods agreement over 75 years ago marked an unprecedented effort of international cooperation to restore economic prosperity after World War Two (WWII). Since then, the global economy has gone through a period of a Golden Age between the late 1940s and the late 1960s, a turbulent crisis in the 1970s that has fundamentally changed the nature of economic policy since the 1980s, a period of market liberalization and financial deregulation between the 1980s and the mid-2000s, and the most devastating economic crisis since the Great Depression that occurred between 2007 and 2010. It has been over a decade since the Great Recession shook the global economy. Its impact has been felt between nation states as well as within societies. Although aggregate trends in many macroeconomic indicators including employment and growth have rebounded from their recessionary lows, they tend to remain below their pre-2007 levels.

Responses to the Great Recession, which were initially focused on fiscal expansion and loose monetary policy and were subsequently followed by fiscal tightening, have exacerbated for society the negative consequences of the 2007 crisis. The livelihoods of many people, even before Covid, suffered from sluggish real wage growth, more unstable employment patterns, and higher costs of living—a legacy of labour market liberalization and the privatization of many public services since the 1980s. After the crisis, the quality of work and state support for financially vulnerable households have deteriorated further as a result of austerity policies which followed the

Julio López Gallardo and Hanna Szymborska, *Do We Need a New Bretton Woods to Tackle the Crisis of Modern Capitalism?* In: *International Equilibrium and Bretton Woods*. Edited by Jerzy Osiatyński and Jan Toporowski, Oxford University Press. © Oxford University Press (2022). DOI: 10.1093/oso/9780192856401.003.0008 wave of bailouts of financial institutions that were at the centre of the Great Recession. Historically low interest rate levels introduced by central banks in advanced economies have failed to stimulate private investment. Instead of pursuing productive investment projects, non-financial firms have expanded their cash holdings and promoted stock buybacks, which can be partly attributed to growing uncertainty about macroeconomic stability. Simultaneously, emerging economies have been struggling with growing balance of payments volatility owing to the requirements of domestic fiscal discipline, free trade, and capital account liberalization associated with multilateral financial assistance from the International Monetary Fund (IMF) and the World Bank.

Despite rising inequality and faltering levels of both public and private investment, economic policy has not turned to radical solutions. By promoting domestic and external market liberalization and restricting government's involvement in the economy to interventions that inherently rely on private markets to bring about recovery, policymakers have favoured the maintenance of the global economic status quo. This institutional arrangement is based on a belief in the superiority of private markets in delivering economic prosperity and has itself contributed to the crisis of modern capitalism. This stands in stark contrast to popular political attitudes, which seem to reflect social discontent with the persistently unequal rewards of the capitalist system. Even more astonishing is the fact that countries which have been key advocates of sustaining the global economic status quo, including the US and the UK, have experienced a shift of political power towards critics of the global economic order based on free trade and capital and labour mobility.

In this light, some speculate whether time has come for a new Bretton Woods system to be established to restore economic and social prosperity in the increasingly fragmented capitalist world. In this chapter, we explore whether ideas for a new international economic system put forward in the 1930s and the 1940s by John Maynard Keynes and Michal Kalecki could be applied to tackling the ongoing crisis of modern capitalism. First, we review Keynes's and Kalecki's original proposals for global economic cooperation after WWII. Second, we examine the merits of these proposals under the conditions of contemporary capitalism, arguing that Bretton Woods solutions cannot be easily transplanted to modern times. The chapter concludes with a discussion of what kind of international cooperation is needed to stimulate the global economy and reduce inequality in the future.

7.2   Proposals for a New International Economic System

Kalecki was well aware of the vital role of the foreign sector and of the availability of international liquidity for the evolution of any economy, and conscious of the importance of coordinated action by different nations for expansionary measures to achieve complete success.[1] Thus, in a very early paper (published under the pseudonym Henryk Braun in a socialist magazine) he put forward the idea that, 'we should mention yet another possibility [to overcome the world crisis of the 1930s], namely ... individual states, or group of states, starting up major public-investment schemes, such as construction of canals or roads, and financing them with government loans floated on the financial market, or with special government credits drawn on their banks of issue' (Kalecki 1932 [1990]: 53). He remarked, however, 'if it were to be carried out on a large scale, it would have to be co-ordinated by an international agreement of the individual capitalist governments, which, given today's quarrelling imperialism, is almost out of the question' (Kalecki 1932 [1990]: 53)[2].

For a time, Kalecki did not elaborate further on the topic. However, during the 1940s, surely stimulated by the debate initiated by Keynes on organization of the post-war system of international trade and finance, he published two short papers where he reflected on the macroeconomic links between nations, both from the point of view of world effective demand and with a proposal to amend Keynes's original scheme. We will discuss these two papers later, but for now it will be appropriate to present in some details Keynes's proposal, and to the extent to which it is possible, in his own words.[3] This will set the stage to clearly understand the debate as well as Kalecki's contribution.

The aim of Keynes's proposal was to encourage expansion rather than contraction, in the sense of a promotion of the international division of labour, and also of facilitating an increase of effective demand in any country

---

[1] The section draws on Lopez and Assous, 2010: ch. 7, 'Kalecki's Open Economy Macroeconomics', pp. 152–73.

[2] One year later, Keynes published in *The Times* a series of four papers, which would later appear as 'The Means to Prosperity' (1933 [1978]. In those papers Keynes argued along similar lines to Kalecki, but with greater optimism. To overcome the world crisis, countries should embark on large-scale loan-financed expenditure, and this would necessitate international co-ordination among leading capitalist countries. Keynes put forward these ideas to influence public opinion, but especially the participants of the World Monetary Conference, organized by the League of Nations in 1933.

[3] Keynes made several versions of his proposal, and we select here paragraphs from that version where it seems to us the ideas are more clearly articulated.

wishing to carry out full-employment policies. He envisioned the situation as follows:

> The problem of maintaining equilibrium in the balance of payments be-
> tween countries has never been solved, since the methods of barter gave
> way to the use of money and bills of exchange ...
>
> To suppose that there exists some smoothly functioning automatic
> mechanism of adjustment which preserves equilibrium if only we trust
> to methods of laissez-faire is a doctrinaire delusion which disregards the
> lessons of historical experience without having behind it the support of
> sound theory.
>
> (Keynes 1978: vol. 25, 21–2)

He then stated the following requirements for a well-functioning new world order:

(a) we need an instrument of international currency having general ac-
ceptability between nations ...

(b) We need an orderly and agreed method of determining the relative
exchange values of national currency units ...

(c) We need a quantum of international currency, which ... is governed by
the actual current requirements of world commerce, and is also capable of deliberate expansion and contraction to offset deflationary and
inflationary tendencies in effective world demand.

(d) We need a system possessed of an internal stabilising mechanism, by
which pressure is exerted on any country whose balance of payments
with the rest of the world is departing from equilibrium in either direction, so as to prevent movements which must create for its neighbours
an equal but opposite want of balance.

(e) We need an agreed plan for starting off every country after the war with
a stock of reserves appropriate to its importance in world commerce ...

(f) We need a method by which the surplus credit balances arising from
international trade, which the recipient does not wish to employ for
the time being, can be set to work ... without detriment to the liquidity
of these balances and to their holder's faculty to employ them himself
when he desires to do so.

(g) We need a central institution, of a purely technical and non-political
character ...

(h) More generally, we need a means of reassurance to a troubled world,
by which any country whose own affairs are conducted with due

prudence is relieved of anxiety, for causes which are not of its own making, concerning its ability to meet its international liabilities.

(Keynes 1978: vol. 25, 168–9)

Keynes then went on to the following proposal:

> The proposal is to establish a Currency Union designated an International Currency Union, based on international bank money, called ... bancor, fixed (but not inalterably) in terms of gold and accepted as the equivalent of gold by all the members of the Union for the purpose of settling international balances. The central banks of all member states ... would keep accounts with the International Clearing Union through which they would be entitled to settle their exchange balances with one another at their par value as defined in terms of bancor ... Measures would be necessary ... to prevent the piling up of credit and debit balances without a limit ...
>
> The idea underlying such a Union is simple, namely, to generalise the essential principle of banking as it is exhibited within any closed system. This principle is the necessary equality of credits and debits. If no credits can be removed outside the clearing system, but only transferred within it, the Union can never be in any difficulty as regards the honouring of cheques drawn upon it. It can make what advances it wishes to any of its members with the assurance that the proceeds can only be transferred to the clearing account of another member.
>
> (Keynes 1978: vol. 25, 170–1)

Finally, Keynes made more precise his proposal by suggesting that each member of the union be given a quota according to its importance in world trade,[4] by defining permissible upper bounds to the debit and credit balances of each member of the union, and by establishing fines that would be charged to both credit and debit balances when the country exceeded its permissible quota in either direction.

Let us now come to Kalecki's reflections on the issue. His first paper, written with E. S. Schumacher, was in direct response to Keynes's and White's plans, and basically suggesting amendments to the former.[5] His

---

[4] The quotas he proposed were quite generous.

[5] The paper was published in a special Supplement to the Bulletin of the Oxford University Institute of Economics and Statistics, devoted to the discussion of these plans. Kalecki and Schumacher, as well as T. Balogh, the other contributor to the Supplement, worked at the institute.

second paper dealt in more general terms with the requirements to make multilateralism workable; that is, the requirements to ensure that any country wishing to carry out full employment measures did not find obstacles to meet its international liabilities. These obstacles could easily arise if countries with a balance of payments surplus simply sterilized their surplus, thus depriving other countries of the requisite international liquidity. We will first consider the second paper, given its more general approach.

In this paper, Kalecki recognized that

> world multilateralism can secure a better utilization of world resources than bilateralism or regional blocks (although in the latter case the difference may not be so great). Nor does multilateralism raise the political issues that may be in the formation of regional blocks. It is therefore superior to other systems provided that it is workable; that is, provided that it is operated under conditions of such a kind that no difficulties in balancing imports of goods and services with exports arise for full-employment countries.
>
> (Kalecki 1946 [1990]): 409–10)

Kalecki then argued that, on one hand, multilateralism would be unworkable if employment in major industrial countries were subject to strong fluctuations. On the other hand, he was sceptical that the trade balance problems of full-employment countries could be solved by introducing trade restrictions or currency depreciation. Trade restrictions would mean 'the failure of multilateralism to secure the international division of labour' (Kalecki 1946 [1990]: 412). Currency depreciation may not solve the situation because under imperfect competition a fall in unit cost need not translate into a reduction in the final price of production if firms decline reducing their mark-ups.

Kalecki finally inquired about the necessary conditions for a viable multilateral system. He showed that if all countries maintained full employment on the basis of a sufficient level of internal demand, then no country would experience difficulties in balancing its foreign trade. However, if some major countries do not achieve full employment but have a great demand for imports, other countries may still reach full employment without difficulties in balancing their foreign trade. The reason is simply that when a country has balanced trade, it is not subtracting international liquidity from other countries. On the contrary, high import demand from major underemployed countries could provide the rest of the world with the requisite international liquidity to carry out their full employment policy. Alternatively, inflationary pressures could be generated if a country has already reached full employment due to their domestic demand conditions.

Kalecki then argued that other possibilities exist to make multilateralism compatible with the pursuit of full employment. He mentioned two cases. The first one would occur when each country maintains

> full employment based on domestic expenditure and on foreign net expenditure financed by long-term loans. Thus, each country must maintain such a domestic expenditure that this expenditure plus export surplus financed by foreign lending (or minus export deficit financed by foreign borrowing) is adequate to assure full employment. Indeed, if a country has an export surplus which is not financed by foreign long-term lending, and if, in accordance with our assumption, it will not do so out of its domestic expenditure [i.e., it will cut it—H.S.], effective demand will exceed the full employment mark and an inflationary situation will arise. To deal with it, the country will have to increase its imports or to reduce its exports, or both. In this way, the surplus which is not financed by foreign long-term lending will be eliminated.
>
> (Kalecki 1946 [1990]: 414)

Another possibility would be the following: 'If some countries are not fully employed, this does not mean that the full-employment countries will necessarily experience difficulties in balancing the proceeds and outlays of foreign exchange. The imports of not fully-employed countries plus their foreign lending may provide the full-employment countries with foreign exchange adequate to cover their imports from the former countries' (Kalecki 1946 [1990]: 414).

Kalecki warned, however, that if these conditions were not met 'a breakdown of pure multilateralism and its replacement by another system of international trade is unavoidable' (Kalecki 1946 [1990]: 416).

In the first paper, co-authored with Schumacher, the authors agreed with the aim and with many of the specific proposals contained in Keynes's plans However, they went beyond that proposal. First of all, they stated:

> There is no merit in a general policy aiming at current account equilibrium for all countries, because different countries are at different stages of economic development, and a regular flow of investment from the more highly developed to the more backward regions of the world may redound to the benefit of all …

Is there, then, any merit in a general policy aiming at what we have called 'unbalanced equilibrium', i.e. at a balance in the current account and the long-term capital account taken together? There is, indeed, a strong case for it ... if 'disequilibrium' destroys the international liquidity of the deficit country ...

If, therefore, the supreme aim of a new international system and a new international policy is to be expansion rather than contraction ... it may be worth while to consider whether the dangers of disequilibrium, which consist of the resulting illiquidity of the deficit countries, could not be overcome by other means [than by inducing the surplus countries to ration their exports and by inducing the deficit countries to ration their imports].

(Kalecki and Schumacher 1943 [1997]: 226–7, emphasis in the original)

The authors therefore imagined a very ingenious mechanism, with three main features. First, 'countries can have any surplus they may like, but will not, by hoarding their surpluses, endanger or ruin the international liquidity of others' (Kalecki and Schumacher 1943 [1997]):227). Second, they distinguished three typologies of countries, according to their level of development and to their international economic position (see below). Third, they suggested attaching an International Investment Board (IIB) to the Clearing Board. We think it is important to describe their proposal in detail.

Kalecki and Schumacher's idea aimed for the following:

(i) to make it possible for any country desiring to have an export surplus to hoard unlimited amounts of gold or bancor ... (ii) to safeguard countries needing an import surplus for purposes of reconstruction, readjustment, and industrialization ['A' countries] against any long-term deterioration in their international liquidity; and (iii) to provide an instrument for international policy by means of which help can be given to countries which cannot be included under (ii) ['B' countries; namely countries whose deficit in the current balance of payments is due to reasons other than those arising in the course of industrialization, reconstruction, or readjustment] to maintain a long-term balance in their current account.

(Kalecki and Schumacher 1943 [1997]: 228)

To carry out this international strategy, they proposed the attachment of an 'International Investment Board to the International Clearing [Union] which decides the amount of long-term loans which might be granted to deficit countries' (229), distinguishing between (i) and (ii) countries.

Moreover, to ease the international situation of 'B' countries the 'Board should have the power to direct borrowers receiving development loans to use them fully or partly to increase their imports from specified 'B' countries' (230).

Nevertheless, the authors concluded their reflection with this warning: 'If investment decisions have to be taken by an international authority, there arises, of course, a political problem of first magnitude ... investment decisions, and decisions directing a borrower to make his purchases in one particular country, involve a high degree of political responsibility' (231).

Unfortunately, the Kalecki–Schumacher proposal did not receive the attention and discussion it deserved. In fact, as we know, even Keynes's proposal was largely abandoned in favour of the plan elaborated by Harry Dexter White, the US Chief International Economist, at the US Treasury in 1942–44[6].

7.3 Bretton Woods Institutions Today

The present goals and operations of the Bretton Woods institutions differs substantially from both Keynes's and Kalecki's original vision. Since the 1980s, the World Bank and the IMF have been leading advocates of policies that reproduce the global economic status quo based on the presumed superiority of private markets over government in stimulating economic activity. This belief has its roots in the neoclassical economic theory, according to which increasing labour market flexibility and liberalizing a country's current and capital accounts has beneficial effects on domestic output and employment.

In particular, the IMF has focused its assistance to poorly performing economies on promoting structural adjustment programmes (SAPs). This policy package has become an important source of financing in crises-stricken economies, particularly those characterized by current account deficits. SAPs provide international financial assistance at concessional repayment terms. In recent history, policymaking in many low- and middle-income countries has become reliant on international finance, including loan assistance from the IMF and the World Bank. This has had a profound

---

[6] Thomas Balogh, the third member of the trio to write in the special Supplement of the Bulletin of the Oxford University Institute of Economics and Statistics previously cited, kept alive for several years the debate on the New International Economic System, as evidenced by his papers collected in Balogh (1963).

impact on the shape of domestic policies in these countries, as access to funds from the IMF and the World Bank has been underpinned by a number of conditions. These include policy requirements of domestic market liberalization, balancing of government budget through fiscal discipline and privatization, current and capital account liberalization, as well as openness to foreign investment, which need to be implemented in the recipient country.

One of the key features of the requirement of domestic market liberalization associated with multilateral financial assistance from the Bretton Woods institutions is downward wage flexibility. Neoclassical economic theory claims that under liberalized current and capital accounts, wage reductions improve a country's competitiveness through currency depreciation, which allows for the expansion of exports and leads to a better trade balance. Improvement in the trade balance raises demand levels in the domestic economy, which absorbs any negative side-effects that the initial fall in wages may have on workers.

Kalecki provides vital insights into the pitfalls of implementing such solutions to stimulate aggregate demand in an open economy. Focusing on the effects of currency depreciation and policies increasing wage flexibility, he shows that aggregate demand need not increase as a result of unit cost reductions. This is because firms operating under imperfect competition would increase their degree of monopoly by raising mark-ups rather than lowering prices of final products.

Other policy requirements related to financial assistance from the Bretton Woods institutions are also unlikely to stimulate aggregate demand. The emphasis on fiscal discipline has been associated with substantial reduction in public spending on vital services such as education, health care, social welfare, and public infrastructure. This has been accompanied by calls for privatization based on sales of state-owned assets to the private sector and increased provision of public services and infrastructure projects through private–public partnerships (PPP). Together, these developments have put upward pressure on the costs of living in low- and middle-income economies and contributed to higher income and wealth inequality within these countries, which has acted to further supress aggregate demand in emerging economies.

Higher income inequality and constrained aggregate demand resulting from domestic market liberalization have been exacerbated by external market liberalization required by the IMF and the World Bank. First, the requirement of capital account liberalization has been associated with greater balance of payments volatility in low- and middle-income countries, sparking numerous currency crises since the 1990s, from Mexico and Argentina to Turkey, India, and South East Asia. Liberalization of international capital flows has opened the door to the possibility of sudden capital flight resulting from international investors' changing perceptions of economic and political stability in emerging economies. Large capital outflows have been followed by sudden depreciation of domestic currencies in these countries, which has deepened balance of payments deficits by making international debt repayments (often denominated in US dollar) more difficult.

Second, the emphasis on current account liberalization as a condition for accessing multilateral financial assistance has done little to boost economic growth in emerging economies. Free flows of goods, services, and finance across borders have been argued to expand consumption and production opportunities in low- and middle-income countries, by providing access to technologies and high value-added goods produced by developed economies in the Global North. However, due to declining terms-of-trade for agricultural products and low-value-added manufactured goods exported by many emerging economies, external market liberalization has exacerbated the dependence of low- and middle-income countries on imports of vital technologies and products from the Global North. Moreover, the experience of current account liberalization has been asymmetric across the developed and emerging economies. Many emerging economies have faced trade barriers on their exports to the Global North, for instance, under the Multifibre Agreement which was implemented between the mid-1970s and mid-2000s. As a result, balance of payments problems have deepened, contributing to greater economic instability in emerging economies.

Furthermore, the requirement of openness to foreign investment (direct and portfolio flows) has not improved domestic capacities for sustained economic growth in low- and middle-income countries. Inflows of foreign direct investment (FDI) have boosted profit opportunities for multinational corporations (MNCs), with the majority of profits from FDI activity in emerging economies being repatriated to the Global North. FDI projects have been primarily export-oriented, meaning that production in the recipient economies has been directed by foreign demand rather than domestic needs. But despite the emphasis on export-led growth, FDI inflows have often required importation of expensive machinery and technology from the Global North, exacerbating balance of payment deficits in low- and middle-income countries. Simultaneously, the presence of MNCs has often provided few opportunities for increased tax revenues due to transfer pricing practices by MNCs and the low tax rates needed to attract FDI in the first place.

Moreover, flows of foreign portfolio investment (FPI) account for a large and increasing share of overall net resource flows to low- and middle-income countries. This has been greatly aided by implementation of the 2030 Agenda for Sustainable Development[7] and other international initiatives such as Maximising Finance for Development (MFD)[8] put forward by the World Bank. These policies have called for greater openness of emerging economies to trade and international financial flows. But similarly to FDI flows, FPI flows have not contributed to supporting domestic aggregate demand. Instead, they have been prone to sudden capital flight due to their short-term nature driven by responsiveness to interest rate differentials around the world.

In sum, the Bretton Woods institutions have undergone a substantial evolution since the time of their founding. Policies advocated by the IMF and the World Bank have been characterized by a shift in priorities and methods, underpinned by the belief in state-minimalism and the benefits of domestic and external liberalization. Consequently, today the Bretton Woods institutions effectively promote a realignment of global economic relations towards private profit-oriented incentives, which does not guarantee that the patterns of economic cooperation remain equitable, and may risk exacerbating inequality between and within countries.

---

[7] Several Sustainable Development Goals (SDGs) express commitments to free trade and free capital flows. For instance, SDG 17 under targets 17.10 and 17.12 aims to promote an open multilateral trading system under the World Trade Organization and implementation of duty-free and quota-free market access for least developed countries (United Nations 2020). While there is recognition of the unequal terms based on which developing countries access the global economy (e.g. under SDG 10, target 10.a, which calls for special treatment of developing countries in international trade), achievement of some of the SDG targets (e.g. SDG 17, target 17.11: a significant rise in the exports of developing countries) seem to contradict the goal of equitable international economic cooperation, for reasons outlined in this chapter.

[8] The MFD agenda was set up in 2018 by the World Bank, aiming to 'systematically leverage all sources of finance, expertise, and solutions to support developing countries' sustainable growth' (World Bank 2020). The MFD agenda promotes securitization and financial innovation in emerging economies to mobilize finance for development projects. In order to attract global financial investors, it encourages domestic financial systems to be restructured towards capital markets by engaging in issuing securities, development of domestic securities markets, and establishment of domestic shadow banks. According to the World Bank, in this way 'private finance can become an option for countries that have not been able to access it because they lack the right institutions or markets' (World Bank 2020). The MFD agenda using securitization will be tested in financing infrastructure projects ('Roadmap to Infrastructure as an Asset Class' document, https://www.oecd.org/g20/roadmap_to_infrastructure_as_an_asset_class_argentina_presidency_1_0.pdf).

7.4 A New Bretton Woods?

Could the Bretton Woods agreement be effective in stimulating economic prosperity around the world today? To answer this question, one needs to consider the economic conditions underpinning international cooperation today and over 75 years ago. As will be argued below, the original Bretton Woods proposals are unlikely to successfully deliver economic prosperity in the modern context. While there are similarities between the state of the global economy then and now, there are marked differences which prevent straightforward application of the Bretton Woods ideas today.

One important similarity between the economic conditions today and in the mid-1940s is low unemployment levels. The original Bretton Woods agreement was set in a context of near full employment levels prevailing globally after WWII. Similarly, by the late 2010s high-income countries experienced near full employment levels as unemployment rates reached their lowest levels since the 1980s. Moreover, the performance of the global economy in the mid-1940s was suffering in the lingering aftermath of the Great Depression, while the global economy in the early 2020s has been shaken by a series of damaging crises: the Great Recession in the late 2000s and the coronavirus pandemic in 2020. The dire economic situation of the global economy strengthens the rationale for international cooperation, as individual countries struggle to contain the long-term negative effects of economic crises on their societies.

Among other similarities, the modern global economy suffers from mounting contradictions related to persistent inequalities. A highly uneven distribution of income and wealth was sustained for several decades preceding WWII and it also became more polarized in the years before the Great Recession (Piketty 2014). However, the nature of inequality has changed over time. At the time of the Bretton Woods agreement disparities in income, wealth, and living standards could be observed between countries due primarily to the different scale of damage resulting from WWII. Nowadays, inequality is predominantly a within-country phenomenon (Milanovic 2016). IAs a result, international economic cooperation faces the challenge of ensuring that integration of countries into the global economy does not deepen domestic inequalities between social classes.

In addition to rising within-country inequality, recent evidence suggests that global inequality has also been increasing. Since the 2010s, household wealth inequality has risen in many economies (Szymborska 2019). Moreover, while inequality in incomes measured at the country level has been falling, this trend has been driven primarily by gains in economic growth in Asia. In fact, the global share of income going to sub-Saharan Africa has been falling (Alvaredo et al. 2018). Furthermore, income disparities remain large among the global population (Hickel 2017). The gap between the share of global income going to the richest 1 per cent and the poorest 50 percent in the world has been widening since the 1980s (Alvaredo et al. 2018).

Rising global inequality exposes another fundamental difference between the conditions underpinning global economic cooperation at the time of the Bretton Woods conference and today. Emerging economies occupy a different position in the international monetary system today compared to the mid-1940s. When the rules of global economic cooperation were being established in 1944, low- and middle-income countries taking part in the Bretton Woods conference had a substantial degree of domestic policy independence, in terms of e.g. regulating capital flows and maintaining fixed exchange rates. At present, countries that wish to participate in the international monetary system need to give up their domestic policy independence in favour of floating exchange rates and balance of payments liberalization.

One important reason behind the lack of domestic policy independence in emerging economies is related to policy conditions required to access multilateral financial assistance from the IMF and the World Bank, which were described in Section 7.3. Nowadays, low- and middle-income countries face greater balance of payments volatility compared to members of the Bretton Woods conference. In contrast to rules of global economic cooperation established in 1944, emerging economies which are part of the international monetary system today have to adopt flexible exchange rates, remove controls on the cross-border flows of goods, services, and finance, and undertake extensive domestic market liberalization based on fiscal discipline, privatization, and labour market flexibility. As a result, Bretton-Woods-style global economic cooperation would occur with highly unequal terms, which would deepen the extractive core-periphery dynamics in the global economy. The call towards greater openness to international capital flows and trade in emerging economies, which was described above, is an example of such unequal integration of the Global South into the global economy.

The unequal nature of international economic cooperation in the twenty-first century is highlighted by stark environmental injustice faced by emerging economies and by the global poor. Global CO_2 emissions have increased exponentially over the past decades, from approximately 5 billion tonnes in 1950 to over 35 billion tonnes in 2017 (Ritchie and Roser

2020). This rise was driven initially by the US and the advanced economies in Europe. But since around the 1980s, Asia, and especially China, have accounted for the largest share of the annual CO_2 emissions around the world. Increasing CO_2 emissions in Asia have been facilitated by high (and rising) foreign demand for Asian exports, particularly in the US and Europe.

Interdependence between the patterns of consumption in the Global North and the intensity of production in the Global South cannot be neglected by the terms of global economic cooperation in the future. Environmental policy efforts aiming to mitigate the negative impact of climate change through imposing additional costs on the largest 'suppliers' of greenhouse gas emissions need to consider the demand side as well. Without that, future international cooperation risks placing a greater burden of dealing with climate change on emerging economies, which tend to have fewer resources to ensure environmentally sustainable growth. This could exacerbate the existing socio-economic inequalities experienced by low- and middle-income countries integrated into the global economy. The existing evidence suggests that the poorest 50 per cent of the global population are responsible for only 10 per cent of total CO_2 emissions related to lifestyle consumption, but that they are more likely to bear the burden of climate change compared to the richest 10 per cent of the global population, who are responsible for nearly half of total lifestyle consumption emissions of CO_2 (Oxfam 2015).

On the whole, a key factor tying the aforementioned disparities between the state of the global economy today and at the time of the Bretton Woods agreement is the type of prevalent economic paradigm which underpins policymaking. The need for rapid large-scale recovery in physical infrastructure after WWII motivated high levels of government spending. And while Keynes's proposal for the International Clearing Union (ICU) based on bancor has not been adopted, the dominant approach to economic policy in the two decades that followed the Bretton Woods agreement was characterized by the Keynesian emphasis on stimulating aggregate demand through expansionary measures. In contrast, it is likely that proposals for Bretton-Woods style global economic cooperation in the present context would be based largely on a neoclassical approach to policymaking focused on fiscal discipline, domestic and external market liberalization, financial deepening within and across countries, as well as maintaining price stability and managing expectations of financial investors through passive rules-based policy measures. Initiatives for international economic cooperation based on such terms would likely exacerbate the existing socio-economic and environmental inequalities between and within countries and act to supress aggregate demand levels in the global economy.

It is not possible to predict accurately what the state of the global economy would be today had the Kalecki-Schumacher proposal been adopted at Bretton Woods. Nevertheless, based on discussions in this chapter, we hypothesize that Kalecki and Schumacher's vision of global economic cooperation had the potential to create a more sustainable and inclusive global economy. Being rooted in a demand-led theory, the Kalecki-Schumacher proposal for the structures of international economic cooperation, especially the amalgamation of the IIB with the ICU, could have perhaps reined in the neoliberal shift of the Bretton Woods institutions in the 1980s. Through highlighting the challenge of political responsibility among international authorities, Kalecki and Schumacher's proposal might also have contributed to a more democratic distribution of power among core and periphery countries within the global economy. Last, by prioritizing full employment, the Kalecki-Schumacher plan might have strengthened aggregate demand, particularly in terms of investment, in countries at different stages of economic development. This could have mitigated the widespread issue of low domestic investment levels and stagnant productivity growth, as well as rising within-country income inequality observed since at least the 1980s.

In sum, the holistic nature of Kalecki and Schumacher's plan—evident in their analysis of international trade and global capital flows and their formulation of appropriate policy responses to address balance of payments problems in countries with deficient demand—might have alleviated to some degree the contradictions faced by the global economy today by explicitly addressing the problem of persistent macroeconomic imbalances between core and periphery countries. This might have improved the present arrangements for international full-employment equilibrium through contributing to the relatively lower scale of global inequality and assisting least-developed countries in breaking away from the cycle of persistent underdevelopment.

7.5 Conclusion

Economic crises are an inherent feature of capitalism. Crises cannot be avoided, but their negative consequences can be alleviated by inclusive macroeconomic policy focused on stimulating aggregate demand. This chapter evaluated the possibility of a new Bretton Woods agreement for international economic cooperation in the context of the secular stagnation and high inequality that have recently been experienced by many countries in the global economy. The chapter reviewed the main proposals for ensuring economic stability through international economic cooperation which were put forward by Michał Kalecki and John Maynard Keynes at the time of the Bretton Woods conference in the aftermath of WWII. The chapter argued that a Bretton-Woods style agreement could not easily be transplanted into the modern context due to several fundamental differences characterizing the state of the global economy today and in the mid-1940s. At present, international economic cooperation faces an overwhelming challenge of radically rethinking the ideological tenets on which the dominant approach to economic policy is based. This would require learning from the insights of Kalecki and Keynes in order to realign policy priorities of international economic cooperation away from the neoclassical emphasis on maintaining price stability and promoting individual profit opportunities towards inclusive stimulation of aggregate demand across the entire global economy. Such an approach would create opportunities for nurturing global economic prosperity that is not only more socially just but also environmentally sustainable.

References

Alvaredo, Facundo, Lucas Chancel, Thomas Piketty, Emmanuel Saez, and Gabriel Zucman 2018 *World Inequality Report 2018*. Available at https://wir2018.wid.world/contents.html, accessed 15 April 2020.

Balogh, Thomas 1963 *Unequal Partners*. Oxford: Basil Blackwell.

Hickel, Jason 2017 *The Divide: A Brief Guide to Global Inequality and its Solutions*. London: William Heinemann.

Kalecki, Michał 1932 [1990] 'Is a Capitalist Overcoming of the Crisis Possible?', in Jerzy Osiatyński (ed.) *Collected Works of Michał Kalecki, Volume 1 Capitalism: Business Cycles and Full Employment*. Oxford: Clarendon Press, pp. 48–53.

Kalecki, Michał 1946 [1990] 'Multilateralism and Full Employment', in Jerzy Osiatyński (ed.) *Collected Works of Michał Kalecki, Volume 1 Capitalism: Business Cycles and Full Employment*. Oxford: Clarendon Press, pp. 409–416.

Kalecki, Michał and Ernst F. Schumacher (1943 [1997]) 'International Clearing and Long-Term Lending', in Jerzy Osiatyński (ed.) *Collected Works of Michal Kalecki, Volume VII Studies in Applied Economics 1940–1967 Miscellanea*. Oxford, Clarendon Press, pp. 226–232.

Keynes, John Maynard 1933 [1978] 'The Means to Prosperity', in Donald Moggridge (ed.) *The Collected Writings of John Maynard Keynes, Volume IX Essays in Persuasion.* Cambridge: Cambridge University Press, pp. 335–366.

Keynes, John Maynard 1978 'The Origins of the Clearing Union, 1940–1942', in Donald Moggridge (ed.) *The Collected Writings of John Maynard Keynes, Volume XXV Activities 1940–1944 Shaping the Post-War World: The Clearing Union.* London and New York : Macmillan and Cambridge University Press, pp. 1–144.

López, Julio, and Michaël Assous 2010 *Michal Kalecki.* New York: Palgrave Macmillan.

Milanovic, Branko 2016 *Global Inequality.* Cambridge, MA: Harvard University Press.

Oxfam 2015 *Extreme Carbon Inequality.* Available at https://www.oxfam.org/en/research/extreme-carbon-inequality, accessed 15 April 2020.

Piketty, Thomas 2014 *Capital in the Twenty-First Century.* Cambridge, MA: Harvard University Press.

Ritchie, Hannah, and Max Roser 2020 'CO$_2$ and Greenhouse Gas Emissions', published online at OurWorldInData.org. Available at https://ourworldindata.org/co2-and-other-greenhouse-gas-emissions, accessed 15 April 2020.

Szymborska, Hanna K. 2019 'Wealth Inequality in the European Union', in Robert Sweeney and Robin Wilson (eds) *Cherishing All Equally. 2019 Report.* Dublin: Think Tank for Action for Social Change.

United Nations 2020 *Sustainable Development Goals Knowledge Platform.* Available at https://sustainabledevelopment.un.org/?menu=1300, accessed 16 April 2020.

World Bank 2020 *Maximizing Finance for Development (MFD).* Available at https://www.worldbank.org/en/about/partners/maximizing-finance-for-development, accessed 16 April 2020.

8

International Debt and the Problem
of Equilibrium

Jan Toporowski

8.1 Introduction

The situation seventy-five years after Bretton Woods is rather different from
the one that faced Keynes and White in Bretton Woods, and Kalecki com-
menting on their plans from the distance of Oxford. The most obvious
difference is, of course, that the Bretton Woods conference took place while
Europe, North America, and East Asia were still at war, so that the planners
were able to define the forthcoming peace in ways that supported their respective proposals. Moreover, all the planners were advising on a world in
which international capital flows were largely under the control of central
banks, and they knew that their governments could largely decide on the
pace at which war-time financial controls were dismantled.

Despite the current nostalgia among certain of Keynes's followers for such
exchange controls, it is unlikely that such controls could be resumed without
a crisis to disarm the opposition of international business and banking circles to any constraints on their international payments. A major difference
between the present situation and that of seventy-five years ago has been
the rise of private (non-government) international debt, described by Noemi
Levy-Orlik in Chapter 5, and alluded to in subsequent chapters by Stephany-
Griffith-Jones, Hanna Szymborska, and Julio López Gallardo. Such debt, and
the private capital flows by which debt stocks are maintained and modified,
cannot easily be brought under the control of governments without joint action, to prevent disputes such as those that prolonged the international debt
crisis of 1982, or the more recent Argentine debt controversies.

We cannot therefore transfer wholesale to our present time the policies
discussed at the time of Bretton Woods. But what we can do is to use the

Jan Toporowski, *International Debt and the Problem of Equilibrium*. In: *International Equilibrium and Bretton
Woods*. Edited by Jerzy Osiatyński and Jan Toporowski, Oxford University Press.
© Oxford University Press (2022). DOI: 10.1093/oso/9780192856401.003.0009

insights that emerged seventy-five years ago to understand better our present situation and the policies that may alleviate the economic problems. This chapter presents a framework of macroeconomic policies derived from the ideas of Kalecki as a means of securing international debt and payments that he regarded as the weak link in the international monetary system.

8.2 The Situation Today

At Bretton Woods, Keynes and White, and in Oxford, Kalecki, were all advising on a world in which international capital flows were largely under the control of central banks. In part this was a response to the breakdown of the gold standard, during and following World War One (WWI). This had resulted in the emergence of currency zones in which multilateralism could operate between members of a currency zone (i.e. income from one country could be used to make payments to another country in the same zone). But payments between currency zones were intermediated by central banks in the financial centres of those zones, which gave priority to sustaining their holdings of gold and foreign currency reserves. A key political influence was World War Two (WWII), during which participating governments had taken control over the foreign assets of the private sector in their respective countries in order to restrict payments to residents in enemy countries, or in territories under enemy occupation, and to concentrate foreign exchange resources on imports essential for the war effort. Kalecki was prescient in at least noting the possibility that private capital flows may come into their own again at some stage (Kalecki 1946 [1990]).

The current economic disequilibrium has the distinctive feature that it arises in a world that is, with significant exceptions (e.g., China, India), integrated into an international financial system based on US dollar credit and debt in which private *financial* payments, as opposed to payments for trade in goods and services, constitute nearly all international foreign exchange transactions. In such a world, international monetary disequilibrium appears as problems of private and government indebtedness in that international financial system. The most exposed part of that system is constituted by commodity export dependent countries, whose financial condition varies with unstable world commodity prices. This dependence does not arise because of some preordained condition of 'underdevelopment', or the absence of thrift in those countries, but because of institutional improvisations introduced to patch up the inadequacies of the Bretton Woods international monetary system, agreed by Keynes and White, as that system went through a series of crises, from the abandonment of multilateralism in 1949, to the collapse of the system of fixed exchange rates in 1976; the international debt crisis of 1982, followed by the emerging market crises of the 1990s; the international banking crisis of 2008, and finally the impact of the Covid pandemic.

Faced with these crises, the Bretton Woods institutions, the World Bank, and the International Monetary Fund (IMF), have done what they were set up to do, namely lend. Their major innovation was the introduction in 1969 of a currency made up of a basket of key currencies in the IMF portfolio (the US dollar, sterling, Japanese yen, Chinese renminbi, and the Euro) and known as Special Drawing Rights (SDRs). Additional allocations have been made at various times, most recently after the 2008 crisis, and recent allocations have been skewed towards poorer countries. At the time of writing there is pressure for a new allocation to assist governments with the payment pressures that have been incurred on account of the Covid pandemic.

However, SDRs may only be held by member governments of the IMF. This certainly eases the pressure on them in their payments to each other. The problem is that they may not be used as payments to non-government or private counterparties. A further limitation of SDRs is the bureaucratic procedure required to issue them. The procedure gives the United States government a veto over their issue which needs agreement by the Board of the IMF. Therefore this is not a procedure that allows for markets to be flooded with liquidity in the event of a crisis. Much more expedient, in the context of domestic financial markets, has been the quantitative easing of central banks since the 2008 crisis. In the context of the international monetary system, the more effective monetary innovation has been the currency swaps set up by the US Federal Reserve, instituted in the 1990s. These are in effect currency repurchase agreements that the Federal Reserve has offered to a select group of other central banks, offering at times unlimited amounts of dollars to be swapped for a foreign currency, and secured by a repurchase agreement under which the dollars are returned to the Fed. But it is the Federal Reserve which announces the names of the central banks that have access to this facility, and those central banks are in the wealthy countries (Canada, Australia, New Zealand, Japan, Europe) and among emerging markets include only Mexico, South Korea, and Singapore. Currency swap agreements have played their part in maintaining a relative stability of exchange rates among key currencies—although this is not the intention of the swaps—and were reinforced in March 2020 to support the financial markets dependent on dollar funding in those countries covered by the agreements. However, the vast majority of countries remain outside this liquidity guarantee. It is their exclusion that renders developing countries the weakest link in the international monetary system.

The following remarks are therefore addressed to those countries, rather than semi-industrialized developing countries with significant manufacturing exports, such as those in East Asia and parts of Latin America. In recent decades, commodity export dependent countries have become integrated into the international financial system, and now face the following circumstances that threaten the sustainability of their governments' debt and fiscal positions:

- low or falling commodity prices. These had fallen by around 20 per cent even before the onset of the Covid crisis in 2020 (IMF 2019: 5). In countries dependent on raw materials exports, this adverse shift in terms of trade brings with it slower economic growth, reduced foreign direct investment (FDI), lower revenue for governments, demands for higher government expenditure, and therefore widening fiscal deficits;
- the prospect of contraction in the liquidity of international financial markets as central banks in Europe and North America move to 'normalize' their monetary policy by ceasing, or reversing, their quantitative easing policies and raising interest rates. Such 'normalization' may seem a distant prospect during the Covid pandemic that has spared no country in the world. But the 'normalization' will certainly feature in policy discussions after the medical emergency. Much like the reinstatement of the gold standard after WWI, a move to restore the monetary consensus that prevailed before the pandemic, or even before the 2008 crisis, may be expected to have a substantial impact on the twin processes that determine the volume of international liquidity today: the willingness of banks to lend against the security of foreign assets, and the willingness of central banks to buy securities. It is such fluctuations in the 'liquidity preference' of banks that were responsible for the turbulence in the New York money markets on the 23 September 2019, just days before the OECD conference from which some of these chapters are drawn. The slow-down in the pace of credit-creation will make it more difficult to roll over existing foreign borrowing, placing the burden of interest and principal repayments on income generated from exports. The prospects for such a credit contraction are still present, despite continued central bank buying of

securities since the emergence of the Covid pandemic, and the renewal of US Federal Reserve swap arrangements with selected central banks in March 2020;

- a large expansion of borrowing in foreign currency by firms in the respective private sectors of many developing countries;
- populist pressures in Europe and North America to reduce official aid to developing countries.

The deterioration in debt sustainability is especially ironic, given the two decades that absorbed the energies and resources of governments around the world and international financial institutions in managing and reducing the foreign debt of the least developed countries. The Heavily Indebted Poor Countries' Initiative was launched by the IMF and the World Bank in 1996, to write-off debts owed by the poorest developing countries. New commitments on foreign debt under the Millennium Development Goals were reinforced by the Multilateral Debt Relief Initiative of 2005, to allow 100 per cent relief on eligible debts owed to the IMF, the World Bank, and the African Development Bank. In 2007, they were joined by the Inter-American Development Bank to provide debt relief to the five Highly Indebted Poor Countries in the western hemisphere. The conditions were sustained commitment to IMF programmes, and policies to combat poverty. By 2020, thirty-six out of thirty-nine potentially eligible indebted poor countries had received US$76 billion in debt service relief (IMF 2021).

Unfortunately, as multilateral debts were being written off, the loose monetary policies of the key central banks in response to the 2008 crisis in the United States—and subsequently in Europe, with near zero interest rates and huge bond purchase programmes under 'quantitative easing'—boosted liquidity in international monetary markets. The result was a sharp increase in foreign borrowing not only in emerging markets, but also by governments of the poorest countries that were benefiting from multilateral debt write-downs. Debt positions were rebuilt as developing countries integrated their national financial systems with the international credit system of the financially advanced economies. A narrative around the deflationary evils of debt was swapped for the older neoclassical argument of a deficiency of 'savings' in poorer countries (Toporowski 2018).

As this indicates, the foreign debt position of developing countries— exposing those countries to serious financial risk arising from any deficiency in foreign currency cash flow, and making those countries the weakest link in the international monetary system—was on the verge of crisis when it was overtaken by an even more serious crisis, the Covid pandemic. In April 2020, the finance ministers of the G20 group of nations agreed a Debt Service Suspension Initiative, under which the debt service payments to the World Bank, the IMF, and other multilateral finance institutions, would be suspended, with effect from the 1 May to the end of 2020. This deadline was subsequently extended through to July 2021. By October 2020, of the seventy-three countries eligible for Debt Service Suspension, thirty-three were close to or in debt distress.

While this initiative provides laudable relief for governments under fiscal strain from the deterioration in their countries' terms of trade, it hardly constitutes the efficient use of credit to support government fiscal programmes, transferring credit into circulation in the real economy. The reasons for this are sunk in the details of debt management rather than in the present value calculations of future obligations: in the cash flows that keep the economy turning over from period to period. Relief from current debt obligations is by no means the same thing as cash revenue available to governments to pay other foreign obligations. Relief from a debt that cannot be paid can hardly bring in cash income that may be used as means of payment for essential imports. And if that relief brings with it a suspension of new lending (the need for debt relief is hardly reassuring for new lenders), the breakdown in capital flows means crisis for foreign payments. Such risk is supposed to be reflected in interest rate margins and not in the suspension of credit supply. Where it frees resources to pay other obligations, it principally benefits middle-income countries whose export revenue constitutes a significant part of national income. Such countries typically have different kinds of foreign debt obligations. Relief from debt obligations to multilateral lenders to such countries, where it does economize on use of foreign revenue, may simply transfer that saving to payments on bilateral debt. This has given rise to tensions between the 'Paris Club' of government lenders to developing countries, and the Chinese government, which offers different terms to governments of poor countries that cannot afford payments on their foreign debt.

8.3 Reforming Institutions and Policy Frameworks: Fiscal Policy

In the present situation, where credit channels are unable to fulfil their function of facilitating and stabilizing fiscal expenditure, it is useful to return to Kalecki's reproach to the participants of Bretton Woods, that they did not take into adequate consideration the economic situation of developing countries, and his recommendation that those countries needed reliable systems of long-term finance (Kalecki and Schumacher 1943 [1993; Kalecki 1946 [1990]). Given the changes that have transformed the international monetary system since the 1940s, what policy and institutional changes are necessary to stabilize the economies of developing countries in order to prevent deterioration of the fiscal and debt position of governments in those countries? Can it be the 'elimination of macroeconomic imbalances' (i.e., fiscal and trade deficits) that is the Mecca of the Bretton Woods institutions, following on from the Keynes or White plans? Or can governments learn the techniques of managing debt in public and private sectors by rebalancing their policy framework in order to maintain stable income and expenditure flows in their respective economies and sustain policies towards the achievement of the Sustainable Development Goals and the Addis Ababa Action Agenda to which governments and multilateral agencies are committed? Such rebalancing cannot be successful if only one instrument, say fiscal policy, or interest rate policy, is dedicated to debt management. A policy framework for debt sustainability and financial stability requires a combination of policies including the following measures.

First of all, governments in developing countries must as far as possible seek to maintain existing (non-financial) expenditure in their economies, in order to prevent a deflationary reinforcement of the reduction in FDI that was already taking place even before the pandemic affected developing countries and their markets in wealthy countries. To compensate for that reduction in FDI, governments should expand public investment, in particular in infrastructure and housing where welfare and economic benefits are large, but import costs are small. Failure to do this will reduce economic growth which in turn will negatively impact upon government tax revenues, so that the prospects of reducing fiscal deficits recede further into the future. This is in addition to the increased expenditure on health and welfare caused by the pandemic.

The inevitable fiscal imbalances need to be addressed by debt management as well as, in the long term, increasing taxation. This is an aspect of fiscal policy that has been incorrectly modelled in developing countries by 'supply-side policies' of lowering taxes and tax incentives that attribute mystical powers of economic invigoration to such actions. In general, such modelling does not take into account cash flows in the economy, with the result that such policies have failed to reduce the dependence of emerging economies on commodity exports or address the housing and infrastructure bottlenecks to economic development. Supply-side policies reduce the tax base of poor countries, by removing taxes on foreign trade, and seeking to replace those taxes by taxes on retail trade, such as value added tax, where the scope for such taxation is limited by popular demand for subsidies or low prices. The overall effect tends to be regressive, since those with higher incomes and wealth tend to import more. A corollary of such tax policies has therefore been the rise in inequalities of income and wealth. This last is a symptom of another feature of developing country economies that is destabilizing public and private finances, namely the growth and concentration of private accumulations of liquid or monetary assets.

Where do these private accumulations of liquid assets come from? The economic process of for-profit production that characterizes free enterprise results in the accumulation of liquid assets (bank deposits or cash) corresponding to the cash profits made from production and exchange. In developing countries, a common consequence of any rise in employment is an increase in the prices of food and basic necessities that then concentrates the accumulation of money in the hands of local farmers and landowners and, in the case of the modern sector of the economy, in the accounts of multinational companies. Primary fiscal deficits and trade surpluses then add to the accumulations in these monetary 'sumps'. They are a cause of financial instability in large part because most developing countries lack the financial markets to tie up this liquidity in financial instruments in the domestic currency. The accumulations then drain out of the economy into foreign, convertible currencies, or do so abruptly when alarms are raised about the prospect of inflation (devaluing the local currency). In the case of foreign-owned funds, this alarm typically arises when companies or funds perceive, or expect, 'macroeconomic imbalances': a combination of fiscal deficits and trade deficits. However, it should be emphasized that it is not these macroeconomic imbalances themselves that directly cause such capital flight. The capital flight cannot take place without monetary accumulations, because it is currencies, and not assets in general, that are traded in foreign exchange markets. In extreme cases, such capital flight can give rise to 'dollarization', as holders of liquid assets convert those assets into foreign currency, and then proceed to use that foreign currency in their transactions between each other. Capital flight on this scale undermines the exchange rate making foreign borrowing more expensive.

The monetary accumulations therefore have important implications for fiscal policy and debt management, as well as the monetary policy (interest rates) that is supposed to keep capital movements in order. Taxation needs to be targeted on accumulations of wealth, not just in order to reduce the liquid assets held by property owners, but also in order to tie up more of that liquidity in the markets for the property that is being taxed. For example, land is an illiquid asset. But a tax on land payable in the domestic currency obliges landowners to keep money in that currency ready to pay the tax, or to borrow in the domestic currency in order to pay that tax. Wealth taxes, and taxes on luxury consumption are therefore an important way in which governments can reduce fiscal deficits, addressing concerns about macroeconomic imbalances, and promote financial development (in the sense of markets in illiquid assets). Contrary to the widespread supply-side narrative, taxes on wealth or luxury consumption do not affect incentives to invest, since these taxes cannot be reduced by lowering investment (Kalecki 1954 [1993]).

8.4 Reforming Institutions and Policy Frameworks: Debt Management

A second important aspect of the policy framework that needs to be addressed to meet the challenge of lower commodity prices and international illiquidity is the question of debt management. Wherever possible, governments should be financing their deficits in domestic currency markets through the issue of financial obligations at the longest possible maturity. Domestic currency debt has the advantage that it is 'hedged' by a government's assets and income in that same currency: government assets in foreign currencies consist overwhelmingly of their foreign currency reserves, rather than revenues that may be varied by decision of their Ministry of Finance. Even where such reserves may be large enough to manage current commitments on total (private and public) foreign debt, they may not be large enough in the event of capital flight or a need to roll over short-term debt.

A second advantage of domestic currency borrowing arises because a government can manipulate the terms of borrowing in its own currency, where the central bank sets interest rates, or through operations along the yield curve if markets are sufficiently developed. A third advantage of government borrowing in its domestic currency is that the issue of longer-term domestic obligations helps to keep monetary accumulations in an economy tied up in domestic financial markets, and therefore less prone to capital flight. When the central bank issues domestic currency reserves against the value of the new foreign currency reserves, it will often sell domestic currency bonds to 'sterilize' the increase in the money supply. This is becoming less common as central banks in developing countries move towards inflation targeting as their policy framework. But there is no reason why a Ministry of Finance, or its debt management office, cannot issue long-term obligations to stabilize wealth portfolios, without infringing the 'independence' of the central bank.

By contrast, foreign currency debt, can easily become a burden on a country's earnings from exports, in particular as those earnings are threatened by low commodity prices. It should be emphasized that it is not only the government's foreign currency debt that poses this threat, but also private sector foreign currency debt. Unless the private sector has assets abroad, its foreign currency debt payments are a claim on the foreign currency reserves of a government that cannot be refused without causing currency devaluation. Devaluation can then dramatically increase domestic resource costs of government foreign currency debt. In general, Kalecki was sceptical about the trade benefits of devaluation, which he considered were largely offset by deterioration in terms of trade implied by devaluation (Kalecki 1933 [1990]). But any limited trade benefits can be more than offset by an increase in the burden of debt denominated in foreign currency.

Needless to say, foreign debt also has important political implications. While it appears to provide free money by not drawing on domestic resources, taxation to service foreign borrowing or the conditions under which external loans are given can easily become a target for political opposition. Taxation and political reform come to be regarded as foreign impositions, weakening the political authority necessary for effective governance. Where governments are already weak or have limited domestic political legitimacy, foreign borrowing further undermines legitimate political endeavour.

Special mention should be made here of the Eurobond borrowing of many African governments in the years before the pandemic. While there is no doubt that such borrowing added to the foreign currency reserves of governments, this is not a *net* addition, but merely the foreign currency counterpart of a new foreign currency liability. Given the suspension of multilateral debt payments for the poorest countries, and the direction of abundant liquidity in international financial markets towards middle-income emerging markets, the possibilities for refinancing this Eurobond debt, within the ten-year maturities of most of these bonds, is precarious. Alternative methods, such as the diaspora bonds that have been pioneered in Africa by Ethiopia and Nigeria, are limited by the wealth of the countries' respective diaspora. Nigeria, for example, raised US$300 million through diaspora bond issues in

2017. But this is a very small fraction of its total or even net Eurobond issue. Another alternative is the issue of foreign currency bonds to domestic residents. Such issues may be useful in draining foreign currency from the economy to prevent dollarization. But again, the amounts that can be raised are insignificant by comparison with government foreign currency debt in general.

An important influence on the fiscal and debt position of governments in poorer developing countries is the foreign aid that they receive from governments in wealthier countries. In the 1950s and 1960s, Kalecki was in general sceptical of the benefits that such aid could provide for developing countries (Kalecki and Sachs 1966 [1993]). Today much of this aid has been enhanced by co-financing with development banks, multilateral agencies, and private sector institutions. Such co-financing increases the dependence of foreign aid on the liquidity of international markets. Private sector participation in co-financing is especially dependent on the possibilities of refinancing. In countries that do not have adequate markets for long-term finance, those possibilities inevitably rest with multinational companies or investment institutions that are willing to hold illiquid assets in poor countries. However, the decline in FDI suggests that this may be difficult and add to the financial problems of developing countries. Nevertheless, it is important that aid flows should continue, and that they should support the fiscal positions of governments in order to avoid the deflationary effects of reduced government expenditure.

This indicates that perhaps the final challenge for developing countries is the absence of an institutional mechanism that could convert foreign currency debt into domestic debt. Such conversion is essential if governments of developing countries are to have control over their debt and the terms on which it is serviced. The matter is made more urgent in view of the devaluation of the US dollar by approximately 20 per cent since the decline in commodity prices set in in 2014. Since many of the imports by developing countries are from Europe and East Asia, this represents an adverse shift in terms of trade of those countries. Although most developing country foreign debt is denominated in US dollars, the change in terms of trade increases the domestic resource cost of that debt.

In financially advanced countries this conversion of foreign currency debt into domestic currency debt is readily effected and has even been institutionalized in the foreign exchange swaps market supported by central bank currency swaps. In emerging markets and developing countries, the Bretton Woods institutions, the IMF, and the World Bank have under fairly strict conditionality participated in arrangements for refinancing government foreign debt, and finally in the writing off of foreign debt since the Highly Indebted Poor Countries Initiative in 1996. But this refinancing has remained in foreign currencies, rather than converting the debt into domestic currency debt. The difference is important because, as indicated in section 8.4, a government's domestic currency debt is managed at that government's discretion. Such debt is therefore more manageable by governments, and its issue contributes to financial development in a way that foreign currency debt does not. Among larger emerging markets (for example in Mexico between 1989 and 1994) such a conversion of government debt into domestic currency debt was made possible by a US government guarantee ('Brady bonds') and a favourable conjuncture in the international financial markets and portfolio capital inflows. However, very few developing countries (in Africa only South Africa, perhaps) have capital markets on such a scale as to absorb such a manoeuvre. In any case, such a conversion through capital markets transfers government foreign debt to the private sector, making that sector even more vulnerable to the depreciation that inevitably follows the reduction in investment that accompanies this kind of expansion in indebtedness. This is an important reason why arrangements for such conversion need to be made in a multilateral official framework.

The remarks in this chapter have generally addressed the question of government domestic and foreign debt. They have not directly addressed the problem of private sector debt whose expansion was identified at the beginning of this chapter, and in other chapters (especially Chapters 5 and 7). This was a key development of the Bretton Woods conference, and is now the central obstacle to any attempt to reinstate any of the plans discussed at that conference, or any of the plans of their critics, Kalecki, Schumacher, Prebisch, and Williams. Private debt is a problem for these plans in part because of (a) the instability of such debt; (b) the hedging of such debt in poorer countries on a day-to-day basis by unstable global commodity prices that drive FDI and hence the business cycle in those countries; and (c) the claim in respect of its foreign debt that the private sector makes in crisis on the foreign exchange reserves of the government. The obvious answer to such difficulties is to encourage local, rather than foreign currency financing of investment. However, there are obvious limits to local financing in the case of imported machinery, equipment, and components. Moreover, monetary policy designed to keep inflation low by stabilizing the exchange rate may prove to be incompatible with local financing, if the private sector finds cheaper finance in foreign currencies.

These private sector difficulties may be partially overcome by effective counter-cyclical government expenditure policy aimed at maintaining high levels of employment, as argued for by Kalecki (see Chapters 1 and 3). Such counter-cyclical policy is not only important to obtain the benefits of human welfare, economic efficiency, and the elimination of poverty that result from high levels of employment. Counter-cyclical government expenditure is also crucial to maintaining private-sector cash flow. This needs to be combined with the management of its domestic debt by the government in such a way as to maintain the liquidity of the banking and financial markets on which the private sector depends. Again, in accordance with Kalecki's recommendations, governments, or their central banks, should issue long-term securities to sterilize the excessive liquidity that arises with high levels of government expenditure, issuing short-term securities to maintain that liquidity if the markets become too 'thin', and using operations along the yield curve (selling bonds to buy short-term bills, or selling bills to buy bonds) in order to control interest rates (Michell and Toporowski 2019; Toporowski 2020).

Governments can manage their domestic financial markets in this way. But, with the exception of the Government of the United States, governments cannot manage conditions in the international monetary system. For those conditions, as Kalecki pointed out, of critical importance is the maintenance of high employment in richer countries and, in particular, in the country at the centre of the international monetary system, the United States, to provide a flow of dollars to foreign net debtors in that currency (Kalecki 1946 [1990]; see also Minsky 1989 and Steindl 1989). A further measure, to complete stabilization, is the extension of the currency swap arrangements of the US Federal Reserve to the rest of the world. This has demonstrated its effectiveness in the wake of the 2008 crisis, and since March 2020. It is perhaps utopian to extend this coverage to the whole world. But regional swap arrangements might be effective, if reinforced by facilities to convert governments' foreign currency debt into domestic currency debt.

8.5 Conclusion

Debt sustainability was recognized as a problem of international finance in Kalecki's work on multilateralism and the Bretton Woods discussions. It is the central issue that links those discussions with concerns about the international financial system seventy-five years later. This question has been neglected in the usual discussions about international monetary policy, concentrating on international payments and exchange rates. At the time of Bretton Woods, Kalecki had criticized the false economy of restricting international monetary reserves (see Chapter 3). In 1946, among the conditions for an international monetary system that would support full employment, he laid out the need for automatic provision of *long-term* financing, to eliminate foreign trade constraint on employment, in particular in developing countries.

Institutions of the system are only slowly catching up with the international monetary needs of capitalism. Today, wealthy countries have financial systems that provide long-term finance for their large capitalist enterprises and, since the 1990s, the Federal Reserve has provided its backing to reinforce the liquidity of that financing with the dollar currency that provides reserves to the international monetary system. Outside wealthy countries, with the exception of the three leading emerging markets, such reinforcement is not available. And even among the beneficiaries of the dollar swaps, their consequence is arguably dollarization of those economies, rather than a strengthening of their domestic monetary systems (see Grahl 2020).

Today's deterioration in the finances of many governments in developing countries and the suspension of international financial liquidity for the poorer countries, at a time of unprecedented liquidity for the financial markets of Europe, North America, and East Asia, threaten the fiscal balances and debt sustainability of those governments. To avoid debt crisis, governments need to rebalance fiscal policy towards maintaining government expenditure, but increasing tax revenue, so that fiscal deficits are reduced without austerity. Foreign aid can support such rebalancing by sustaining government expenditure, but might also increase dependence on unstable private capital flows. Government debt is particularly problematic in developing countries, where the international financial system encourages excessive reliance on unreliable foreign borrowing. Domestic borrowing offers more scope for debt management, which can form the basis of domestic financial institutions.

To assure their effective participation in the international monetary system, developing countries need an effective, multilateral mechanism to assure the conversion of foreign government debt into obligations in domestic currency. This last will require support from international financial institutions, including not just financial support, but also a change in their operating procedures. The Bretton Woods institutions need to put into effective practice their stewardship of the world's moneys, instead of just looking after the money of wealthy countries.

Reform of the international monetary system must start from a reconsideration of the fault lines of the present system. Kalecki was remarkably prescient in seeing the fault lines of the system in his time: the dependence of international payments on each country's foreign trade balance and the direction of capital flows, leading to deflationary pressures that create unemployment and the resulting fear and loathing of international cooperation and free trade. He also identified the elements necessary for an efficient international payments system, to back up free trade and multilateralism. The uneven distribution of productive capital around the world means that countries cannot get to full employment without trade deficits destabilizing capital flows. Such trade deficits cannot be overcome by monetary means— adjustments in interest rates, exchange rates, or reserves of international money, operating as a unit of account and a store of value.

Full employment therefore lies at the heart of the political case for multilateralism. Full employment needs to be achieved not only by Keynesian fiscal expenditure. Local deficiencies of productive capital must be addressed by long-term investment planning to secure full employment in the long term. Such investment needs long-term credit. The state can organize the provision of such credit, through state banks or the development banks, discussed elsewhere in this book by Stephany Griffith-Jones (Chapter 6; see also Gerschenkron 1962). This works for domestic payments, but leaves international payments at the mercy of the trade balance. This was recognized by Keynes and White, who agreed on the establishment of an international investment bank, which became the International Bank for Reconstruction and Development. But this falls short of what Kalecki recognized as a structural need for automatic provision of long-term credit to cover the industrialization-related foreign trade payments of developing countries.

In the absence of such a facility, the international monetary system has become institutionally a dollar currency area, in which credit in American currency is used for payments within the area, and a decreasing part of the world is where international payments may be effected without using the US dollar (see Grahl 2020). Developing countries on the margins of the dollar currency area need either continuous access to long-term credit in US dollars, or a facility for translating their dollar obligations into domestic currency on terms that do not threaten their monetary stability, or prospects of development. This is Kalecki's challenge to Bretton Woods.

Acknowledgements

This chapter draws on its author's report on fiscal policy and debt sustainability in Africa for the United Nations Economic Commission for Africa (Toporowski 2018). The author is grateful to Hanna Szymborska for assistance with that report, and to Jerzy Osiatyński for comments on and corrections to an earlier draft.

References

Gerschenkron, Alexander 1962 'Reflections on the Concept of "Prerequisites" of Modern Industrialization', in *Economic Backwardness in Perspective*. Cambridge, MA: The Bellknap Press of Harvard University Press, pp. 31–51.

Grahl, John 2020 'Dollarization of the Eurozone?' *New Left Review* 125(Sep/Oct), pp. 19–33.

IMF (International Monetary Fund) 2019 *World Economic Outlook Global Manufacturing Downturn, Rising Trade Barriers*. Washington, DC: IMF, October.

IMF (International Monetary Fund) 2021 'Debt Relief under the Heavily Indebted Poor Countries (HIPC) Initiative', *Factsheet*. Washington DC: IMF, 18 February.

Kalecki, Michał 1933 [1990] 'On Foreign Trade and "Domestic Exports"', in Jerzy Osiatyński (ed.) *Collected Works of Michał Kalecki Volume I Capitalism: Business Cycles and Full Employment*. Oxford: Clarendon Press.

Kalecki, Michał 1946 [1990] 'Multilateralism and Full Employment', in Jerzy Osiatyński (ed.) *Collected Works of Michał Kalecki Volume I Capitalism: Business Cycles and Full Employment*. Oxford: Clarendon Press.

Kalecki, Michał 1954 [1993] 'The Problem of Financing Economic Development', in Jerzy Osiatyński (ed.) *Collected Works of Michał Kalecki Volume V Developing Countries*. Oxford: Clarendon Press.

Kalecki, Michał and Ernst F. Schumacher 1943 [1993] 'International Clearing and Long-Term Lending', *Bulletin of the Institute of* Economics and Statistics Oxford Supplement 5(7 Aug): 29–33, in Jerzy Osiatyński (ed.) *Collected Works of* Michał Kalecki Volume V Developing Economies. Oxford: Clarendon Press.

Kalecki, Michał, with Ignacy Sachs 1966 [1993] 'Forms of Foreign Aid: An Economic Analysis', in Jerzy Osiatyński (ed.) *Collected Works of Michał Kalecki Volume V Developing Countries*. Oxford: Clarendon Press, pp. 61–91.

Michell, Jo, and Toporowski, Jan, 2019 'Can the Bank of England Do it? The Scope and Operations of the Bank of England's Monetary Policy' *Working Paper* London: Progressive Economy Forum 12 November.

Minsky, Hyman P. 1989 'Financial Structures, Indebtedness and Credit', in Alain Barrère (ed.) *Money, Credit and Prices in Keynesian Perspective*. London: Macmillan, pp. 49–70.

Steindl, Josef 1989 'Saving and Debt', in Alain Barrère (ed.) *Money, Credit and Prices in Keynesian Perspective*. London: Macmillan, pp. 71–78.

Toporowski, Jan 2018 'Fiscal Policy and Debt Sustainability in Africa'. Report for the United Nations Economic Commission for Africa, October.

Toporowski, Jan 2020 'Debt Management and the Fiscal Balance', *Review of Political Economy* 32(4): 596–603.

Index